Howland Island
National Wildlife Refuge

Comprehensive Conservation Plan

Prepared by:

U.S. Fish and Wildlife Service
Pacific Remote Islands
National Wildlife Refuge Complex
Box 50167
Honolulu, Hawaii 96850

Approved: _____   Sept 24 2008
       Regional Director, Region 1   **Date**

Howland Island National Wildlife Refuge
Comprehensive Conservation Plan
Approval Submission
U.S. Fish and Wildlife Service, Region 1

In accordance with the National Wildlife Refuge System Administration Act, as amended, the U.S. Fish and Wildlife Service completed a Comprehensive Conservation Plan (CCP) for Howland Island National Wildlife Refuge (Refuge). The purpose of this CCP is to specify a management direction for the Refuge for the next 15 years. The goals, objectives, and strategies for improving Refuge conditions—including the types of habitat we will provide, partnership opportunities, and management actions needed to achieve desired conditions—are described in the CCP. The Service's preferred alternative for managing the Refuge and its effects on the human environment, are described in the CCP as well.

This CCP is submitted for the Regional Director's approval by:

_____   9/11/2008
Don Palawski, Project Leader   Date
Pacific Remote Islands National Wildlife Refuge Complex

Concur:_____   9/11/2008
Barry Stieglitz, Project Leader   Date
Hawaiian and Pacific Islands
National Wildlife Refuge Complex

Concur:_____   9/16/08
Forrest Cameron   Date
Refuge Supervisor

Concur:_____   9/16/08
Carolyn Bohan   Date
Regional Chief, National Wildlife Refuge System

FINDING OF NO SIGNIFICANT IMPACT

Howland Island National Wildlife Refuge
Comprehensive Conservation Plan
Unincorporated U.S. Territory, Central Pacific Ocean

The U.S. Fish and Wildlife Service (Service) has completed the Comprehensive Conservation Plan (CCP) for Howland Island National Wildlife Refuge (Refuge). The CCP will guide management of the Refuge for the next 15 years. The CCP describes the Service's preferred alternative for managing the Refuge and its effects on the human environment.

Decision

Following comprehensive review and analysis, the Service selected Alternative B in the Environmental Assessment (EA) for implementation because it is the alternative that best meets the following criteria:

- Achieves the mission of the National Wildlife Refuge System.
- Achieves the purposes of the Refuge.
- Will be able to achieve the vision and goals for the Refuge.
- Maintains and restores the ecological integrity of the habitats and plant and animal populations on the Refuge.
- Addresses the important issues identified during the scoping process.
- Addresses the legal mandates of the Service and the Refuge.
- Is consistent with the scientific principles of sound wildlife management.
- Can be implemented within the projected fiscal and logistical management constraints associated with the Refuge's remote location.

As described in detail in the CCP and EA, implementing the selected alternative will have no significant impacts on any of the natural or cultural resources identified in the CCP and EA.

Public Review

The planning process incorporated a variety of public involvement techniques in developing and reviewing the CCP. This included three planning updates, meetings with partners, and public review and comment on the draft planning documents. The details of the Service's public involvement program are described in the CCP.

Conclusions

Based on review and evaluation of the information contained in the supporting references, I have determined that implementing Alternative B as the CCP for management of Howland Island National Wildlife Refuge is not a major Federal action that would significantly affect the quality of the human environment within the meaning of section 102(2)(C) of the National Environmental Policy Act of 1969. Accordingly, the Service is not required to prepare an environmental impact statement.

This Finding of No Significant Impact and supporting references are on file at the Pacific Remote Islands National Wildlife Refuge Complex, 300 Ala Moana Blvd, Room 5-211, Honolulu, Hawaii 96850, and the U.S. Fish and Wildlife Service, Division of Planning and Visitor Services, 911 NE 11th Avenue, Portland, Oregon 97232. These documents can also be found on the Internet at http://pacific.fws.gov/planning/. These documents are available for public inspection. Interested and affected parties are being notified of our decision.

Supporting References

U.S. Fish and Wildlife Service. 2007. Howland Island National Wildlife Refuge: Draft Comprehensive Conservation Plan and Environmental Assessment.

U.S. Fish and Wildlife Service. 2008. Howland Island National Wildlife Refuge: Comprehensive Conservation Plan.

_____
Regional Director

Sept. 24, 2008
_____
Date

Table of Contents

APPENDICES

LIST OF FIGURES

Chapter 1: INTRODUCTION

Introduction

This document is a Comprehensive Conservation Plan (CCP) for Howland Island National Wildlife Refuge (Howland). It will guide management of refuge operations, site visitation, and habitat restoration for 15 years. Guidance within the CCP is in the form of goals, objectives, strategies (Chapter 3), and wilderness study findings (Appendix F). The CCP was revised as appropriate based upon public comments. The refuge manager of the Pacific Remote Islands National Wildlife Refuge Complex (Remotes Complex) in Honolulu, Hawaii, is responsible for implementing the CCP.

The U.S. Fish and Wildlife Service

Howland is managed by the Fish and Wildlife Service (Service), within the U.S. Department of the Interior. The Service is the primary Federal entity responsible for conserving and enhancing the Nation's fish and wildlife populations and their habitats. Although the Service shares this responsibility with other Federal, State, tribal, local, and private entities, the Service has specific trust resource responsibilities for migratory birds, threatened and endangered species, certain anadromous fish, certain marine mammals, coral reef ecosystems, wetlands, and other special aquatic habitats. The Service also has similar trust responsibilities for the lands and waters it administers to support the conservation and enhancement of all fish and wildlife and their associated habitats.

National Wildlife Refuge System

President Theodore Roosevelt established Pelican Island, Florida as the first national wildlife refuge in 1903. Since that time, the number of refuges has expanded to include 548, totaling approximately 100 million acres. These refuges, found in every state and several U.S. Territories, are administered collectively as a national system of lands with the specific mandate of managing for "wildlife first." This System is the largest collection of lands specifically managed for fish and wildlife conservation in the Nation and perhaps the world. The "wildlife first" mandate of the System means the needs of wildlife and their habitats take priority on refuges, in contrast to other public lands that are managed for multiple uses. The following is a description of some of the most relevant acts and policies that guide the management of the System.

National Wildlife Refuge System Administration Act of 1966, as amended

The NWRS Administration Act defines a unifying mission for all refuges, including a process for determining compatible uses on refuges, and requiring that each refuge be managed according to a CCP. The NWRS Administration Act expressly states that wildlife conservation is the priority of System lands and that the Secretary shall ensure that the biological integrity, diversity, and environmental health of refuge lands are maintained. Each refuge must be managed to fulfill the specific purposes for which the refuge was established and the System mission. The first priority of each refuge is to conserve, manage, and if needed, restore fish and wildlife populations and habitats according to its purpose. The Service has statutory authority under the NWRS Administration Act to regulate activities that occur on water bodies "within" a refuge. The NWRS Administration Act requires a CCP be completed for each refuge and that the public has an opportunity for active involvement in plan development and revision. It is Service policy that each CCP is developed in an open public process.

National Wildlife Refuge System Mission and Goals and Purposes (601 FW1)

In July 2006, the Service issued a policy (601 FW 1) which included the NWRS mission statement and NWRS goals, and described how refuge purposes are determined.

The NWRS Administration Act established the following statutory mission for the System:
"The mission of the System is to administer a national network of lands and waters for the conservation, management, and where appropriate, restoration of the fish, wildlife, and plant resources and their habitats within the United States for the benefit of present and future generations of Americans."

The administration, management, and growth of the System are guided by the following goals (601 FW 1, July 2006)…."

- Conserve a diversity of fish, wildlife, and plants and their habitats, including species that are endangered or threatened with becoming endangered.
- Develop and maintain a network of habitats for migratory birds, anadromous and interjurisdictional fish, and marine mammal populations that are strategically distributed and carefully managed to meet important life history needs of these species across their ranges.
- Conserve those ecosystems, plant communities, wetlands of national or international significance, and landscapes and seascapes that are unique, rare, declining, or underrepresented in existing protection efforts.
- Provide and enhance opportunities to participate in compatible wildlife-dependent recreation (hunting, fishing, wildlife observation and photography, and environmental education and interpretation).
- Foster understanding and instill appreciation of the diversity and interconnectedness of fish, wildlife, plants, and their habitats.

Lastly, the NWRS Administration Act describes refuge purposes, and how these guiding principals for the refuge are located and documented.

Appropriate Refuge Uses (603 FW1)

This policy (603 FW 1), published in July 2006, provides a national framework for determining appropriate refuge uses. Serving as a "prescreening" for proposed uses of a refuge prior to a compatibility determination (see below); this policy requires—for most uses—a written finding of appropriateness by the refuge manager based on 11 criteria. Findings of appropriateness require State concurrence for refuges located within State boundaries. These criteria include:

- Promotes safety of participants, other visitors, and facilities.
- Promotes compliance with applicable laws, regulations, and responsible behavior.
- Minimizes or eliminates conflicts with fish and wildlife populations or habitat goals or objectives in a plan approved after 1997.
- Minimizes or eliminates conflicts with other compatible wildlife-dependent recreation.
- Minimizes conflicts with neighboring landowners.
- Promotes accessibility and availability to a broad spectrum of the American people.
- Promotes resource stewardship and conservation.
- Promotes public understanding and increases public appreciation of America's natural resources and our role in managing and protecting these resources.
- Provides reliable/reasonable opportunities to experience wildlife.
- Uses facilities that are accessible and blend into the natural setting.
- Uses visitor satisfaction to help define and evaluate programs.

Compatibility (603 FW2)

Lands within the System are different from other multiple-use public lands, in that, with few exceptions, they are closed to all public access and use unless specifically and legally opened (603 FW 2). No refuge use may be allowed unless it is determined to be compatible. A compatible use is one that, in the sound professional judgment of the refuge manager, would not materially interfere with or detract from the fulfillment of the mission of the Service or the purpose of the refuge. The NWRS Administration Act identifies six wildlife-dependent recreational uses: hunting, fishing, wildlife observation, photography, environmental education, and interpretation. When compatible, these six uses become priority uses of the System. As priority public uses, they receive special consideration over other general public uses in refuge planning and management.

Biological Integrity, Diversity, and Environmental Health (601 FW3)

The NWRS Administration Act directs the Service to "ensure that the biological integrity, diversity and environmental health of the System are maintained for the benefit of present and future generations of Americans..." This policy (601 FW 3) is an additional directive for refuge managers to follow while achieving refuge purpose(s) and System mission. It provides for the consideration and protection of the broad spectrum of fish, wildlife, plants, and their habitat resources found on refuges and associated ecosystems. When evaluating the appropriate management direction for refuges, refuge managers would use sound professional judgment to determine their refuges' contribution to maintenance and, where possible, restoration of biological integrity, diversity, and environmental health (BIDEH) at multiple landscape scales. Sound professional judgment incorporates field experience, knowledge of refuge resources, refuge functions within an ecosystem, applicable laws, and best available science, including consultation with others both inside and outside the Service.

Wilderness (602 FW 3)

Service planning policy (602 FW 3) requires the conduct of a wilderness review in association with the development of a refuge CCP. The wilderness review process has three phases: inventory, study, and recommendation. After first identifying lands and waters that meet the minimum criteria for wilderness during the inventory phase, the resulting wilderness study areas are further evaluated to determine if they merit recommendation from the Service to the Secretary of the Interior (Secretary) for inclusion in the National Wilderness Preservation System. A more complete discussion of wilderness inventory, study, and recommendation is included in Appendix F.

General Guidelines for Wildlife-Dependent Recreation (605 FW1)

This set of policies (605 FW 1-7), published in July 2006, defines the System's wildlife-dependent recreation policy, provides guidelines used to manage wildlife-dependent recreation on refuge lands and identifies visitor service standards.

National Wildlife Refuges in the Pacific

Nineteen individual refuges are scattered across the central and western Pacific Ocean, with several refuges located on the main Hawaiian Islands and others found from Guam to American Samoa (Figure 1.1). The Hawaiian and Pacific Islands NWR Complex which provides administrative guidance and oversight for the 19 refuges, is located in Honolulu, Hawaii. This Complex also co-manages the newly established Papahānaumokuākea Marine National Monument with the National Oceanic and Atmospheric Administration and the State of Hawaii.

Within this administrative structure is a subset of seven refuges known as the Remotes Complex. The Remotes Complex straddles the Equator near the center of the Pacific Ocean. They are farther from human population centers than any other U.S. area and represent one of the last frontiers and havens for fish and wildlife in the World. These remote refuges are the most widespread collection of coral reef and seabird/shorebird protected areas on the planet under a single country's jurisdiction. Only one of these seven refuges, Palmyra Atoll NWR, has on-island dedicated staff members. Remotes Complex staff, located within the complex office in Honolulu, manage all the remaining refuges, including Howland. Staff, funding, and logistical support are often shared among these remote refuges to help defray operational costs.

The Howland CCP identifies several management strategies that are dependent upon activities and staff support from the Remotes Complex office, ship transportation support from other Federal agencies, or the establishment of partnerships with other organizations. Because of the great distances involved in traveling to these remote refuges, most management activities, including the simple act of visiting a refuge, are sometimes planned to occur concurrently during the same voyage. For this reason, cost estimates for management activities at Howland are pro-rated amongst the seven refuges within the Remotes Complex.

Figure 1.1 Map of National Wildlife Refuges in the Pacific.

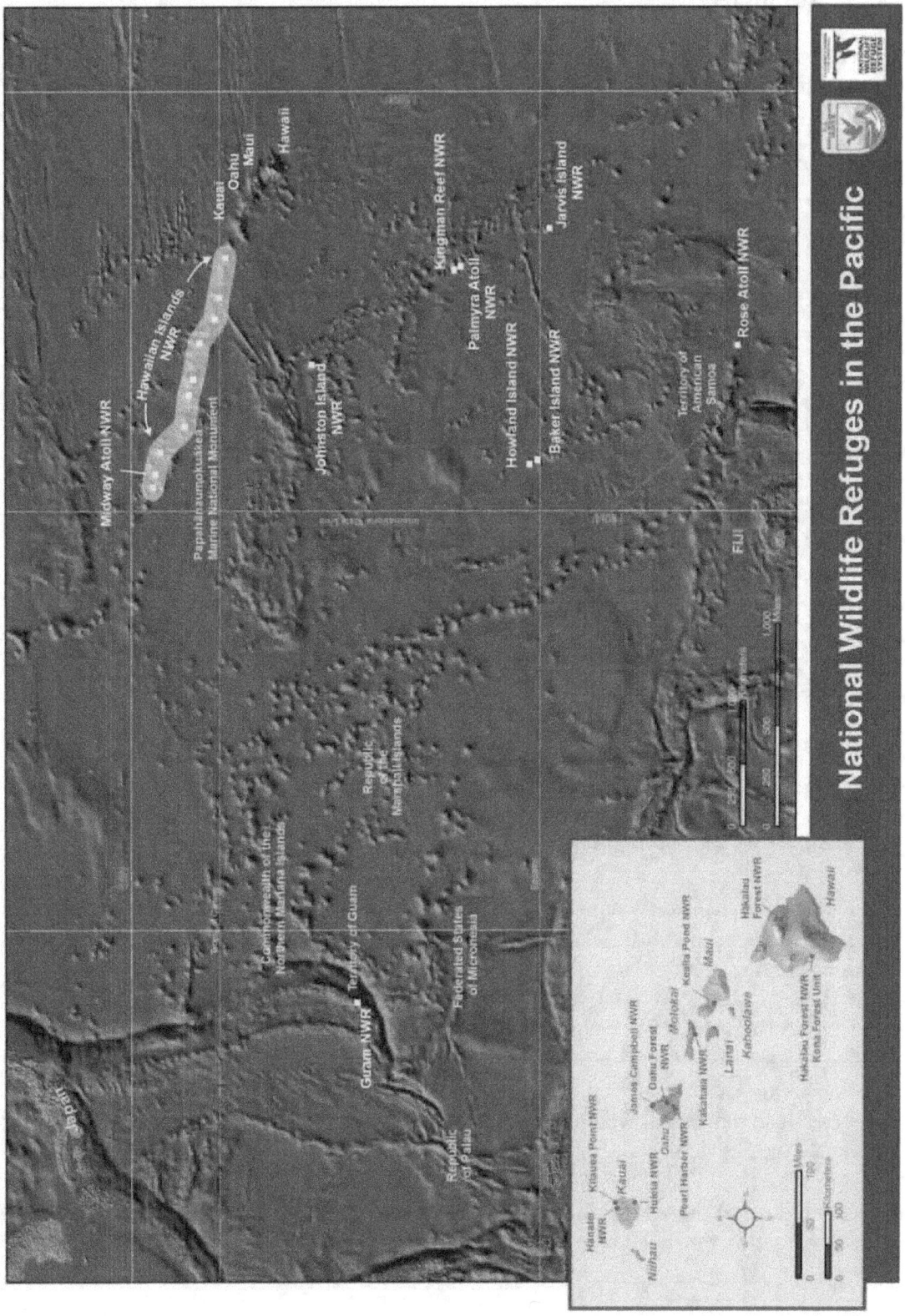

Refuge Establishment, Purpose, and Boundary

Refuge Establishment

Howland Island is an unincorporated territory under the sovereignty of the United States. The Secretary of the Interior has broad authority over the territories of the United States by virtue of the Act of March 1, 1873, (43 U.S.C. 1458) which transferred general authority "...to perform all duties in relation to the Territories of the United States..." from the Secretary of State to the Secretary of the Interior. In addition, President Franklin D. Roosevelt signed Executive Order 7368 on May 13, 1936, also placing control and jurisdiction of Howland Island with the Secretary of the Interior. Further, pursuant to the provisions of the Reorganization Act of 1949, the Secretary of the Interior is authorized under Reorganization Plan No. 3 of 1950 to re-delegate to any officer or agency within the Department of the Interior any of the functions legally under his jurisdiction.

Under the authority of Reorganization Plan No. 3, the Secretary of the Interior, on June 27, 1974, designated Howland Island and its territorial sea extending to the 3 nautical mile (nmi) limit as a unit of the National Wildlife Refuge System to be "administered under the general regulations for the National Wildlife Refuge System published in Title 50, Code of Federal Regulations" (39 FR 27930). Section 25.21 of these regulations state that "...all areas included in the National Wildlife Refuge System are closed to public access until and unless we open the area for a use or uses in accordance with the National Wildlife Refuge System Administration Act of 1966 (16 U.S.C. 668dd-668ee), the Refuge Recreation Act of 1962 (16 U.S.C. 460k-460k-4) and this subchapter C." Howland Island National Wildlife Refuge remains closed to public access.

Refuge Purpose

Refuge purposes are often times are based upon land acquisition documents and authorities. These statements give indications for the biological reason or justification for the acquisition or land transfer. Purposes listed in acquisition authorities, or legislative acts, are often general in scope. For Howland, this general purpose is:

> "...for the development, advancement, management, conservation, and protection of fish and wildlife resources..." (16 U.S.C. 742f (a)(4)), and "...for the benefit of the United States Fish and Wildlife Service, in performing its activities and services. Such acceptance may be subject to the terms of any restrictive or affirmative covenant, or condition of servitude..." (16 U.S.C. 742f (b)(1)) (Fish and Wildlife Act of 1956).

Acquisition documents often contain more specific purpose statements. The specific purpose statement for establishment of Howland identified in the biological ascertainment report at the time of transfer to the Service is (USFWS 1973):

> "...the restoration and preservation of the complete ecosystem, terrestrial and marine. Special consideration must be given to the protection of nesting seabird populations."

Refuge Boundary

Howland is located in the central equatorial Pacific Ocean (Figure 1.2). The boundary for Howland includes:

"all of said island … together with its territorial sea extending outward to the three-mile limit" (39 Federal Register 27930).

The emergent land area for Howland encompasses 648 acres and submerged lands and waters within the 3-mile limit encompass 33,671 acres for a total of 39,319 acres.

Figure 1.2 Howland Island National Wildlife Refuge: Geographic Location and Boundary.

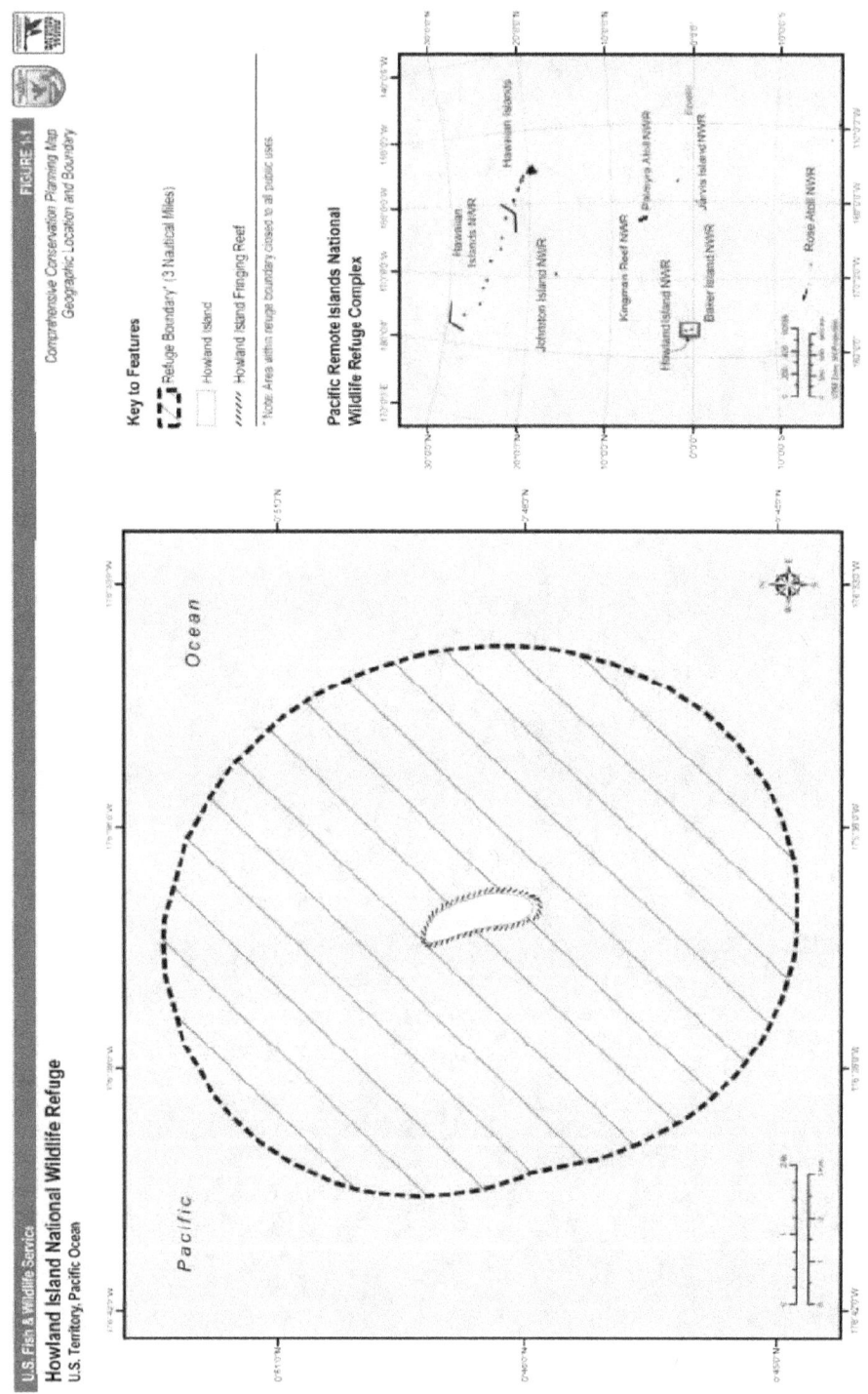

Regional and Ecosystem Conservation Plans

Regional and ecosystem conservation plans and initiatives are also important to evaluate and incorporate into developing each CCP. These plans typically address issues or concerns that are site specific or of regional concern, and address needs more current than when the refuge was established.

Remote Islands Ecosystem Plan: Howland Island, Baker Island, and Jarvis Island National Wildlife Refuge

The ecosystem plan for Howland, Baker, and Jarvis identifies Howland as having a reef that is "…healthy and provides habitat for giant clams" (USFWS 1998b). The plan further implies that all three islands represent models of intact ecosystem components that are either pristine in nature, have been, or are being managed and restored to pre-human contact conditions.

Coral Reef Initiative in the Pacific: Howland Island, Baker Island, and Jarvis Island National Wildlife Refuges

The Coral Reef Initiative for Howland, Baker, and Jarvis restates the wildlife and ecological values identified in the ecosystem plan (USFWS 1998a). This document identifies three important components of the three ecosystems: "They provide a breeding platform for pelagic birds using large areas of ocean surface, offer a migratory stopover for long distance migrating shorebirds, and furnish reef habitat for shallow water organisms."

Recovery Plan for U.S. Pacific Populations of the Hawksbill Turtle (*Eretmochelys imbricate*) (NMFS and USFWS 1998)

Although theoretically within the range for hawksbill turtle, little is known about their biology, foraging and nesting behavior, threats, and distribution surrounding Howland Island. Both the National Oceanic and Atmospheric Administration's National Marine Fishery Service (NMFS), and the U.S. Fish and Wildlife Service share responsibility at the Federal level for the research, management, and recovery of Pacific marine turtle populations under U.S. jurisdiction.

Recovery Plan for U.S. Pacific Populations of the Green Turtle (*Celonia mydas*) (NMFS and USFWS 1998)

Few green turtles are known to forage in the waters surrounding Howland Island and nesting is not known to occur. However, data from the area is limited and use of Howland may be greater than currently documented. Both the NMFS and the Service share responsibility at the Federal level for the research, management, and recovery of Pacific marine turtle populations under U.S. jurisdiction.

U.S. Pacific Island Regional Shorebird Conservation Plan (Engilis and Naughton 2004)

This regional shorebird plan identifies Howland as being within the Central Pacific Islands Subregion. No natural wetlands are known from this subregion; however, beaches on uninhabited islands are important for shorebirds. Population and habitat goals for this subregion state that determining population size and trends for bristle-thighed curlews and other shorebirds, and their habitats is a management priority.

United States Shorebird Conservation Plan (Brown et al. 2000)

This nationwide shorebird plan identifies the U.S. Pacific Islands being of "critical importance for two species of Holartic breeders, bristle-thighed curlew and Pacific golden-plover." Further, this plan notes that these islands provide wintering habitat essential to the maintenance of these species as well as several other migratory shorebird species.

Seabird Conservation Plan, Pacific Region (USFWS 2005)

This plan provides an overarching review, discussion, and identification of conservation priorities for seabirds in the U.S Pacific Islands; ranks seabirds for conservation priority; and includes specific species accounts including their conservation needs.

Central Pacific World Heritage Project

The United Nations Educational, Scientific and Cultural Organization (UNESCO) organized and convened meetings in Honolulu in June 2003, and Kiritimati Atoll in October 2004, to seek input for a proposed multi-national World Heritage project now referred to as the Central Pacific World Heritage Project (CPWHP) (UNESCO World Heritage Centre, 2003; 2004). Additional meetings and evaluations in the U.S. and Republic of Kiribati resulted in a total of 29 atolls, islands, and reefs belonging to four nations (United States, Cook Islands, Republic of Kiribati, and French Polynesia) being proposed for the multi-site, multi-jurisdictional CPWHP. To date, the Service has not acted on this proposal, but may do so in the future. However, in 2006 the Republic of Kiribati established the world's largest marine protected area to date that encompasses all eight of the nation's Phoenix Islands and intended for nomination as a World Heritage site in 2009. All eight are the closest neighbors to Howland and Baker National Wildlife Refuges, lying 200-450 km to the southeast of both islands.

Refuge Vision Statement

The refuge vision statement is a broad general statement that describes what the refuge staff perceives as Howland's fundamental attributes and contributions to a healthy world environment. This statement will guide management activities for the lifespan of this plan, as well into the near future. The vision statement for Howland is as follows.

Howland is one of the last places in the world where the terrestrial and marine tropical island ecosystems are still intact and relatively free of human impacts. Natural, physical and ecological processes unfold with limited human interference and support a diverse community of native marine organisms including seabirds, marine mammals, turtles, fish, plants, corals, and other invertebrates. Nesting and foraging seabirds dominate the landscape and seascape while sheer isolation and solitude help us see our place in the natural world.

Refuge Goals

Goal statements are succinct statements of a desired future condition of refuge resources. Goals comprise the whole of a refuge's effort in pursuit of its vision and lay the foundation from which all refuge activities arise. The goals for Howland are as follows, and will again be presented along with objectives and strategies in Chapter 3.

1. Conserve, manage, and protect native terrestrial habitats that are representative of remote tropical Pacific islands, primarily for the benefit of seabirds.

2. Conserve, manage, and protect native marine communities that are representative of remote tropical Pacific Islands.

3. Contribute to the recovery, protection, and management efforts for all native species with special consideration for seabirds, migratory shorebirds, federally listed threatened and endangered species, and species of management concern.

4. Protect, maintain, enhance, and preserve the wilderness character of Howland's terrestrial and marine communities.

5. Howland's biological, cultural and historic resources are preserved.

6. An informed, interested, and educated public appreciates remote Pacific Island NWRs wilderness values, cultural and historical resources, and their ecosystems, with special emphasis on seabirds.

Chapter 2: PLANNING, PURPOSE, NEED, AND ISSUES

Planning Process

The CCP development process follows applicable policies contained within the Service's Fish and Wildlife Manual (Part 602 FW2.1, November 1996; Part 601 FW1, Part 603 FW1, and Part 605 FW1, June 2006), and the Wilderness Act of 1964 with respect to wilderness study and review. This CCP was completed in association with an EA and is intended to meet the dual requirements of compliance with the NWRS Administration Act and the National Environmental Policy Act (NEPA). Both the NWRS Administration Act and NEPA require the Service to actively seek public involvement in the preparation and adoption of environmental and conservation documents and policies. Furthermore, NEPA also requires the Service to consider a reasonable range of alternatives including its Preferred Alternative and the "No Action" alternative; the latter defined as continuation of current management practices.

Purpose and Need

Overall, all refuges must comply with the System mission, goals, and policies, as described in or promulgated by the National Wildlife Refuge System Administration Act of 1966 (NWRS Administration Act), as amended (16 U.S.C. 668dd-668ee). The National Wildlife Refuge System Improvement Act of 1997 amended the NWRS Administration Act. According to the NWRS Administration Act, a CCP is required to identify and describe refuge purpose(s), habitats and wildlife, archaeological and cultural values, administrative and visitor facilities, management challenges and their solutions, and opportunities for compatible wildlife-dependent recreation. The recreational activities referenced in the NWRS Administration Act as receiving special consideration during planning efforts include hunting, recreational fishing, wildlife observation, interpretation, environmental education, and photography.

The purpose of this CCP is to develop a vision, goals, and objectives for Howland, which in turn provide guidance to identify and implement management activities, or strategies, during the next 15 years. Specifically, the CCP:

- sets a long term vision;
- establishes wildlife and habitat management goals and objectives;
- establishes goals and objectives for compatible wildlife-dependent recreational and educational uses;
- identifies strategies for habitat enhancement and restoration projects;
- describes the highest monitoring and research priorities; and
- describes and evaluates wilderness values.

Howland and its management and administrative activities are managed as part of the NWRS or System within a framework provided by legal and policy guidelines. The refuge is guided by the mission and goals of the NWRS, the purpose of the refuge as described in its acquisition authority, Service policy, Federal laws and executive orders, and international treaties.

Supplemental guidance documents (e.g., resource plans) are also included in making management decisions but cannot replace or be in conflict with the purposes for which the refuge was established or the mission of the System

Planning Issues and Opportunities

Issues, concerns, and opportunities were identified through discussions with key contacts, core team members, other refuge staff, and through the public scoping process. The following section summarizes issues, concerns, and opportunities from all public input received throughout the planning efforts. Six issues were identified and are described below.

Issue 1: Operational Limitations

Howland is located approximately 1,815 nmi from the management staff located in Honolulu, Hawaii. On average, it takes 8 days to reach Howland by ship, the only method of visiting the island. The key issues and concerns affecting planning and management implementation are:
- distance from refuge headquarters;
- lack of affordable and reliable transportation;
- lack of infrastructure to support field operations;
- extreme environmental conditions; and
- safety concerns and logistical capacity to land people and equipment on-island from small boats during limited time windows associated with low surf conditions.

Issue 2: Biological and Ecological Resources

Biological and ecological information sufficient for management or conservation purposes is lacking. Due to the infrequency and limited staff time spent on Howland, biological and ecological information does not allow for a detailed assessment of resources. The collection of baseline and long-term monitoring information should be a primary concern and the focus of management objectives.

Issue 3: External Forces

The threat of the introduction of invasive species from unauthorized visits, marine debris washing ashore and onto coral reefs, and vessel groundings are beyond current management control. Distance, lack of funds and staff, and the inability to have a more consistent presence on this island opens the opportunity for invasive species introductions, limits the ability to remove marine debris, and delays response to vessel groundings.

Global climate change (see Chapter 4) may also affect refuge resources, but is beyond control of refuge management staff. It is anticipated that changes in the chemical composition of the atmosphere and oceans; surface temperatures of air, land, and sea; intensity and frequency of rainfall and storm waves; and changes in sea level would have impacts on refuge resources.

However, the extent and nature of these impacts, if any, is unclear and the subject of considerable academic debate.

Issue 4: Public Use Resources

The key issues related to public use are:
- adverse ecological impacts (invasive species introductions, sewage pollution, fuel spills, trash disposal, harassment of wildlife, damage to sensitive habitats such as coral reefs);
- whether any on-site public use should be allowed;
- to what extent the use should occur; and
- how the use should be managed.

Howland has never been formally opened to public access and use. In the past, several recreational user groups such as amateur radio operators, bird watchers, history enthusiasts, destination tourists, and commercial cruise vessels have expressed interest in visiting various remote Pacific island refuges. Public access to Howland would be managed through use of refuge-issued Special Use Permits (SUP). However, before a SUP could be issued, a request for public access would need to be evaluated for appropriateness and compatibility.

Issue 5: Education and Outreach

In general, Pacific Island refuges are poorly recognized by the public and our partner agencies. There are few entrance signs, no boundary signs, and little published information in popular literature. Refuge boundaries are rarely portrayed on nautical charts and other maps.

The remote location and isolation of Howland and other Pacific island refuges make it difficult to conduct on-site visits for educational or interpretative purposes. Thus, most educational and interpretative opportunities are necessarily delivered remotely through various media.

In addition, general interest by the public and requests to visit remote Pacific Island refuges by a growing recreational yachting community has increased recently. This interest requires the public to be better informed regarding sensitive refuge habitats, species, and regulations.

Issue 6: Communication and Cooperation

Howland's remoteness compels a growing list of partners and cooperators to be kept informed of and included in planning and management activities at Howland. Activities that staff and partner agencies/organizations share include:
- expedition planning;
- collaborative research projects; and
- jurisdictions of trust resources.

Most access for refuge staff to Howland has only been possible through the cooperation and participation with partner agencies such as NOAA and the U.S. Coast Guard. Many research interests are shared between Service and NOAA scientists, and collaborative research projects have been conducted in the past. Additionally, NOAA and the Service share trust resource responsibilities for marine turtles.

Chapter 3: MANAGEMENT DIRECTION

Overview

The Service reviewed and considered a variety of resource, logistic, social, and economic aspects important for managing the refuge when developing this long-term management plan. As is appropriate for a National Wildlife Refuge, resource conditions were fundamental in designing the CCP. Marine and terrestrial resources are equally important to the management of Howland, and are described more fully in Chapter 4. However, the logistics of reaching the island and associated coral reefs is the primary constraint on increasing or modifying the level of management and monitoring activity that has or currently occurs. To more fully understand this constraint, a description of the logistical requirements and refuge management activities follows.

Marine vessels capable of traveling the open ocean for extended periods are the only opportunity for transportation to Howland. In the recent years, NOAA, the U.S. Coast Guard, and private charter vessels have all provided transportation. A typical voyage originating from Honolulu, Hawaii will take approximately 8 days to arrive at Howland excluding intermediate stops at Palmyra Atoll or Johnston Atoll NWRs. Once on-site, if wind and wave conditions warrant the launch of a landing vessel (typically a small outboard type inflatable boat), the marine vessel will anchor or remain stationary during the deployment of the field camp, only venturing away from the island to complete marine surveys. The field camp itself generally consists of two individuals, typically biologists to carry out biological surveys and other duties, and camping gear consisting of tents, sleeping equipment, food, water, and needed survey equipment. Cooking gear is rarely deployed since staff is only on-island for 1 to 2 days with most of that time being engaged in work activities.

While on-island, the biologists document all bird species present, count individuals, determine the stage of any nesting efforts, qualitatively describe vegetation, and record species presence or absence, noting in particular the presence of any invasive species. Observations regarding the condition of cultural sites such as the Amelia Earhart day beacon are also made. The only active management that occurs during these site visits is the collection and on-island stockpile of marine debris that washes ashore and poses a threat to seabirds and other wildlife that use Howland. Any evidence of illegal activity such as unauthorized access is documented. Photographs record general habitat conditions; however, further habitat assessment does not occur. Although no specific activities occur with respect to wilderness values, the simple fact that a 1 to 2 day field camp consisting of temporary lodging arrangements and minimal activity is consistent with maintaining the wilderness values of the area.

During the period that the biologists are on Howland, marine scientists from NOAA, the Service, and other partner organizations such as the University of Hawaii conduct surveys and monitoring activities of the marine environment. Some monitoring activities occur on-board the vessel, while others require the use of SCUBA equipment. All of the marine scientists, however, deploy from the vessel conducting independent marine surveys using other skiffs and thus do not come ashore. Marine scientists typically collect information on currents, weather, temperature, chemical composition of the water, and the abundance and distribution of coral, algae, and other invertebrate and fish species. Specific marine-based surveys known as Rapid Ecological Assessments (REA) are conducted and collect ecological data such as fish species, abundance, and predator prey relationships. Data are also collected at permanently marked coral transects established in 2000-2002 that document changes in coral species, age, size, numbers, and percent cover over time. These data are collected over a 2-day period (six 1-hour dives). Following the voyage, data from marine scientists are provided to the Service that includes a full range of oceanographic, bathymetric, and marine biological information.

Specific details of the management program are categorized below:

- *Baseline Monitoring of Wildlife Populations and Habitats.* Staff visits to Howland provide baseline and temporal monitoring efforts, documenting species presence or absence, abundance, habitat condition, presence of invasive species and various other physical variables such as temperature, precipitation, wind, etc.
- *Voyage Preparation.* The logistics of providing adequate field camp supplies such as water, food, first aid, and communications occurs for each voyage.
- *Use of extraneous unnatural lighting.* Limiting and shading the lighting on vessels, camp, and nighttime operations minimizes the threat of collision and disorientation of wildlife that can be caused by light hazards.
- *Quarantine protocols and use of Integrated Pest Management (IPM).* Visitors to Howland are required to wear new and frozen clothing and other quarantine precautions as outlined in quarantine protocols (Appendix E). Manual pulling of weeds occurs as time becomes available. Selective hand spray application of herbicides or pesticides, where appropriate, may occur.
- *Scientific Information Exchange.* Refuge staff currently attends various professional meetings and conferences related to Pacific island and marine resources. Additionally, a limited amount of staff time is devoted to the development of peer reviewed journal articles and contributing to NOAA and Service-sponsored Web sites and status reports.
- *Preservation of Wilderness Values.* Since its establishment, Howland has been managed to preserve its wilderness values and characteristics even though it has never been proposed for wilderness designation. These values are intrinsic at this remote, uninhabited island and coral reef ecosystem. Management activities do not impinge on these values.
- *Public Access.* Since establishment, Howland has never been formally opened to public access and use. Access and public use remains closed. All individual opportunities for compatible use such as specific research projects are administered using individual SUPs.
- *Interpretation, Education, and Outreach.* Current opportunities for off-site education exist at the Maritime Museum, Honolulu, Hawaii. A hands-on exhibit representing a Pacific island refuge is maintained to educate school-aged students about seabirds, invasive species, marine debris, and the National Wildlife Refuge System (System). Interpretative displays are also used periodically at conventions and professional meetings.
- *Protection and Preservation of Cultural Resources.* Cultural resources remain intact and in situ. Field camps are situated to avoid impacts to cultural resource sites. Archaeological reconnaissance to avoid impacts to cultural resources is required prior to management activity that would potentially disturb surface or subsurface resources.

- *Waste Disposal at Sea.* Disposal of waste in refuge waters is prohibited.
- *Waste Disposal on Island.* All waste from food products, equipment, and containers that is brought onto the island is removed during demobilization. Depending upon the duration of the site visit, human excrement will be either bagged, stored in a chemical toilet, or decomposed using portable biodegradable toilets, all of which are subsequently removed during field camp demobilization.
- *Refuge Boundary.* There are no changes to the refuge boundary.
- *Cultural Resources Inventory.* Presence and condition of cultural resources on *Howland* is re-evaluated.
- *Wilderness Study Area.* A recommendation for Wilderness Study Area (WSA) designation is postponed until a Legislative Environmental Impact Statement (LEIS) and wilderness proposal are developed for all other remote Pacific island national wildlife refuges (NWRs) as part of their CCP processes.
- *Marine ecosystem monitoring.* Funding requests are required for additional exploration of deep slope resources by a ship equipped with a remotely operated vehicle (ROV) or submersible to operate at depths between 150 and 300 feet.
- *Seabird Nesting Restoration.* Electronic calls are deployed and used as seabird nesting attraction devices designed to attract Phoenix petrels (*Pterodroma alba*) and Polynesian storm petrels (*Nesofregetta fuliginosa*). These electronic call devices consist of solar powered speakers broadcasting calls of both species in suitable areas of the island. Both of these small ground-nesting Procellariforms are severely depleted or extirpated throughout much of their range. The mammal-free status of Howland Island makes it an ideal site within the species' original range to restore a breeding population of each species.

Once field operations are complete, or the weather becomes increasingly inclement, the field camp is demobilized and all equipment and personnel are transported back to the research vessel. Typically, the other two other equatorial island refuges (Baker and Jarvis) are also visited in this same manner. Travel time between Howland and Baker is 5 hours, and between Baker and Jarvis is 5 days. Once the three surveys are completed, or at least attempted, the voyage continues with approximately 6 to 7 days to travel back to Honolulu, again with intermediate stops at Palmyra Atoll or Johnston Atoll NWRs, or continuing on for 4 days to Rose Atoll NWR in American Samoa where voyage scientists and biologists can be exchanged and then fly back to Honolulu. In total, it is expected that in order to visit Howland, Baker, and Jarvis for 1 to 2 days per refuge, a biologist or marine scientist needs to devote 20 to 26 days total travel. Trip reports are completed, distributed, and filed once field staff returns to the Honolulu office.

The only difference between the management condition prior to the completion of the CCP, and the actions described in this CCP is an increase in the frequency of staff visits from once every two years to once every year. In order to meet the increase in the number of site visits, refuge staff in Honolulu is administratively burdened to seek additional funding sources and develop partnerships for additional visits. This may take the form of producing internal project proposals (RONS), or seeking funding support through grants or partnerships with other agencies, research institutions, and non-government organizations. Overall, wildlife and habitat management activities remain consistent. The only additional terrestrial management activity is promoting nesting use by two seabird species with the use of solar powered electronic calling devices.

Phoenix petrel calls would be placed near the kou (*Cordia subcordata*) grove, and the Polynesian storm-petrels calls would be placed near the coral slab habitat on the north beach crest. Increased monitoring in the marine environment depends upon partnership opportunities developed with NOAA, the University of Hawaii, or other partners. At a minimum, marine scientists would resurvey REA and other transect sites. Transportation to and from the island would still relies upon NOAA or other partners. Public use and access remains closed.

The ability of the Service to meet the mission of the System, "…to administer a national network of lands and waters for the conservation, management, and where appropriate, restoration of the fish, wildlife, and plant resources and their habitats within the United States for the benefit of present and future generations of Americans" and the refuge purpose of "…the restoration and preservation of the complete ecosystem, terrestrial and marine. Special consideration must be given to the protection of nesting seabird populations" is limited. A one to two day visit to the island once every year does not provide the opportunity for refuge staff to complete anything other than basic biological surveys of species presence or absence. Restoration, preservation, or protection of terrestrial and marine ecosystems, or nesting seabirds is not possible. However, lack of projected budget and staffing preclude management staff from increasing management activity beyond what is described in this CCP. If, during the lifetime of this plan, budget and staffing become available to pursue an increased level of management activity then the CCP will be reevaluated.

Goals, Objectives, Strategies, and Rationale

Goals and objectives are the unifying elements of successful refuge management. They identify and focus management priorities, resolve issues, and link to refuge purposes, Service policy, and the Refuge System Mission.

A CCP describes management actions that help bring a refuge closer to its vision. A vision broadly reflects the refuge purposes, the Refuge System mission and goals, other statutory requirements, and larger-scale plans as appropriate. Goals then define general targets in support of the vision, followed by objectives that direct effort into incremental and measurable steps toward achieving those goals. Finally, strategies identify specific tools and actions to accomplish objectives.

The goals for Howland over the next fifteen years under the CCP are presented on the following pages. Each goal is followed by the objectives that pertain to that goal. The goal order does not imply any priority in this CCP. Some objectives pertain to multiple goals and have simply been placed in the most reasonable spot. Similarly, some strategies pertain to multiple objectives. Following the goals, objectives, and strategies is a brief rationale intended to provide further background information pertaining to importance of an objective relative to legal mandates for managing units of the NWRS including refuge purpose, trust resource responsibilities (federally listed Threatened and Endangered species and migratory birds), and maintaining/restoring biological integrity, diversity, and environmental health.

Goal 1: Conserve, manage, and protect native terrestrial habitats that are representative of remote tropical Pacific islands, primarily for the benefit of seabirds.

Objective 1a: Conserve, manage, and protect habitat for nesting seabirds.
Upon CCP approval and throughout the life of the CCP, conserve, manage, and protect a mosaic of approximately 648 acres of terrestrial habitat consisting of 30 acres of beach and beach strand, 500 acres as short grass and forbs, 6 acres as scrub shrub, and 112 acres as bare ground on Howland Island as nesting habitat for ≥ 11 seabird species.
Strategies Applied to Achieve Objective
Conduct and record incidental observations of invasive terrestrial species.
Adhere to strict quarantine protocols for all island visitors (see Appendix D).
Collect and stockpile marine and other human debris not considered to be historically important.
Rationale:
The 11 nesting seabird species on Howland use all island habitats (see Chapter 3.9.1 and Appendix B). Masked and brown boobies prefer to nest on bare open ground. Gray-backed, sooty, and white tern, and brown and blue grey noddy also nest on the surface, but are tolerant of vegetated areas. Lesser frigatebirds, typically known as a shrub nesting species, are found exclusively on the ground at Howland. Red-tailed tropicbirds prefer shaded areas and can be found nesting on the surface, under coral slabs, or in shrubs. Red-footed booby and great frigatebird are the only two exclusive shrub nesting species. The Seabird Conservation Plan (2005) recognizes remote Pacific islands as providing important and varied breeding habitat, specifically Howland as being important for ground nesting species. Additionally, the plan recognizes that near-shore waters provide areas of upwelling currents with important food resources for seabirds. Maintaining the island free of mammalian predators, invasive insects, and invasive plants is critical for seabird survival (USFWS 2005). Strict quarantine protocols have been previously established for all island visitors in order to eliminate the threat of introducing invasive plants, insects, and animals (see Appendix D). Marine and other human generated debris poses an entanglement threat for multiple wildlife species. Stockpiling debris can reduce the overall area impacted, thereby reducing the entanglement threat.

Objective 1b: Increase baseline information on terrestrial habitat.
Within 15 years of the CCP approval, conduct monitoring to determine vegetation species presence/absence and distribution on Howland Island.
Strategies Applied to Achieve Objective
Document presence/absence of island vegetation.
Coordinate with Regional Office GIS staff to assess and/or develop remote sensing capability to map and monitor island habitats.
Rationale:
In general, insufficient time has been spent on Howland to adequately quantify habitat on Howland, and how this habitat relates to seabird biology. Collection of baseline biological

information is essential to adequately understand and manage the refuge. Although it is known that the 11 nesting seabird species use all habitats on Howland, this information has only been obtained from the short duration, infrequent visits (1 to 2 days every 2 years) to the island. There has been no quantitative assessment of breeding species habitat associations. The distribution and delineation of habitats itself has been estimated, but never been quantified. Remotely collected data may provide an option for data collection in the absence of being capable of visiting Howland.

Goal 2: Conserve, manage, and protect native marine communities that are representative of remote tropical Pacific islands.

Objective 2a: Conserve, manage, and protect marine habitat.
Upon CCP approval, conserve, manage, and protect approximately 33,671 acres of submerged lands consisting of an estimated 3,000 acres coral reef and 30,671 acres of deep water/pelagic habitat on Howland.
Strategy Applied to Achieve Objective
Continue and expand partnership with NOAA and others to manage coral reef ecosystems.
Rationale:
The conservation and protection of the Nation's coral reefs is becoming increasingly important for agencies with responsibility to manage and conserve those (Executive Orders 13089 and 13158). Because the refuge boundary for Howland extends to 3 nmi from the island shoreline, all shallow water coral reefs are contained within the refuge boundary. Threats to the coral reef system include predatory species such as crown-of-thorns starfish, invasive species such as the corallimorph *Rhodactis howesii*, and marine debris (e.g. abandoned fishing gear) that collects on corals, smothering or breaking them. The responsibility for protecting, managing, and conserving coral reef ecosystems is shared with NOAA. The Service and NOAA often participate in joint management activities throughout the Pacific; however, no active management activities have occurred at Howland.

Objective 2b: Increase baseline information on marine community.
Within 15 years of CCP approval, continue monitoring coral species to determine size, cover, density, diversity, and distribution; fish species presence/absence and habitat associations; sea turtle species presence or absence; and marine mammal species presence or absence; oceanographic conditions in relation to climate change effects.
Strategies Applied to Achieve Objective
Conduct and record incidental observations of corals, fish, turtles, marine mammals, and their habitats.
Accompany NOAA or other scientific partners on marine surveys.
Conduct REA (Rapid Ecological Assessments) on at all existing survey sites to document coral, fish and turtle density, diversity, distribution, and habitat associations.
Develop proposals and conduct deep slope marine surveys by ROV (remotely operated vessel) or submersible to document presence or absence of deep slope coral and fish species.
Rationale:
Responsibility for managing marine resources is shared with NOAA, and has led to many cooperative studies. Unlike the logistic constraints of completing terrestrial surveys, marine surveys are conducted throughout the entire time that the marine transport vessel is at Howland.

Additionally, since most site visits to Howland are aboard NOAA research vessels, the purpose of these voyages is to conduct marine surveys and studies. Consequently, a full compliment of up to 20 marine researchers and another 20 support staff contribute to conducting marine surveys across all alternatives. As a result, marine surveys are more comprehensive than terrestrial surveys on Howland, although individual dives are limited to one hour and depths less than 20 m.

REAs constitute baseline monitoring of the marine ecosystem, and are one component of all alternative strategies. Further expansion of REA's could be accomplished only as a component of Alternative D.

Additional surveys (marine mammals, deep slope), as described beginning with Alternative B can be achieved as components of cooperative efforts with other agencies or research organizations. As an example, little is known of marine mammal use surrounding Howland, or the history of sea turtle use and nesting, although it is known that some species are found in the vicinity.

The Marine Mammal Commission has encouraged the Service to generate partnerships with NOAA to help document baseline information. Developing additional partnerships with NOAA or other organizations may also assist in meeting terrestrial objectives by providing the opportunity for additional trips to Howland.

Goal 3: Contribute to the recovery, protection, and management efforts for all native species with special consideration for seabirds, migratory shorebirds, federally listed threatened and endangered species, and species of management concern.

Objective 3a: Develop baseline migratory bird and other species information.
Within 10 years of CCP approval, conduct monitoring (in rank order) to determine: seabird species presence or absence, relative abundance, breeding chronology, distribution, and habitat use; counts of shorebirds; presence or absence and distribution of sea turtles; and presence or absence of terrestrial invertebrates on Howland Island. The desired conditions by which this will be met is understanding of the complete annual chronology for 5 of 11 seabird species; population trend data over the 10-year period for all 11 seabird species; and the numbers and distribution of shorebirds, turtles and other terrestrial invertebrates.
Strategy Applied to Achieve Objective
Record incidental observations of all species' presence or absence, relative abundance, and distribution.
Rationale:
The Seabird Conservation Plan (2005) repeatedly recognizes the importance of the U.S. Pacific Islands in providing predator-free seabird nesting and roosting environments. Their protected status, in concert with nearby marine forage resources contribute to their importance. The Seabird Plan further identifies infrequent inventories as insufficient to accurately detect or monitor populations, suggesting instead that a rigorous collection of population data is needed.

In addition to Howland being recognized as important habitat for seabirds, the U.S. Pacific Islands Regional Shorebird Conservation Plan (2004) lists determining baseline information for bristle-thighed curlews, and other species, as the goal of the Central Pacific Islands Subregion. The endangered species recovery plans for both species of turtles indicate that little is known about their biology in the central Pacific. Data on other terrestrial wildlife species found on Howland Island is lacking.

Objective 3b: Restore breeding populations for 2 seabird species.
Within 10 years of CCP approval, establish up to 5 nesting pairs each of Phoenix petrel (*Pterodroma alba*) and Polynesian storm-petrel (*Nesofregetta fuliginosa*) during a minimum of three consecutive years on Howland Island.
Strategies Applied to Achieve Objective
Implement and maintain electronic calling devices to promote nesting.
Coordinate with RO and develop capabilities for remote surveillance equipment.
Rationale:
The Seabird Conservation Plan (2005) recognizes the Polynesian storm-petrel may flourish on Howland, as well as Baker and Jarvis, due to the removal of predators from the islands. The Phoenix petrel is known from the Phoenix Islands, but does not currently inhabit Howland, though it is thought that they did historically. A recommendation of the Seabird Conservation Plan (2005) is expand efforts to assess habitat suitability and restore populations through translocation to predator-free U.S. islands such as Howland. While the physical translocation of species to Howland is not being suggested, electronic calling devices are designed, and have been successful, in attracting and establishing nesting seabird colonies to other islands.

Objective 3c: Develop baseline data and understand turtle use of Howland.
Upon CCP approval, monitor hawksbill and green turtles to document any nesting sites, all adjacent coral reef and nearshore water foraging sites, and overall population density and distributions, and review literature to determine previous records of, and use of sea turtles during the guano mining and WWII eras.
Strategies Applied to Achieve Objective
Record incidental observations of nearshore turtle use.
Develop partnership with NOAA for study of turtles at Howland.
Rationale:
There is currently little information related to use of Howland resources by sea turtles, though it is known that they do use refuge habitats. Sea turtles may have been collected or harvested during the guano and WWII eras. Sea turtles have been photographed in the water during joint Service/NOAA expeditions since 2000. Data collected over the life of this plan would help to establish a baseline understanding of sea turtle populations in the central Pacific.
Objective 3d: Expand baseline information on marine community.
Upon CCP approval, monitor populations of globally depleted marine species such as giant clams (*Tridacna* sp.), bumphead parrotfish (*Bolbometapon muricatum*), Napoleon wrasses (*Cheilinus undulatus*), large groupers (*Cephalopholis* sp., *Epinephelus* spp., *Variola* spp., etc.), sharks (*Carcharhinus* spp., *Triaenodon* spp., *Negaprion* spp., *Galeocerdo* spp., etc.), pearl oysters (*Pinctada margaritifera*), the invasive corallimorph (*Rhodactis howesii*) and corals (Anthozoa, Hydrozoa) to document their presence or absence and relative abundance on Howland.

Strategies Applied to Achieve Objective
Conduct marine surveys such as REA.
Maintain the monitoring of permanent coral and macro-invertebrate transects established in 2000-2002.
Solicit partnership for survey of deep slope habitat.
Rationale:
Many marine species of commercial importance have been globally depleted. Protected areas such as Howland still provide sanctuary areas. However, illegal fishing activity, including evidence thereof, has been noted surrounding several Remotes refuges. Howland, as well as other remote island refuges provide the opportunity to study and protect the marine ecosystem.

Objective 3e: Develop baseline scientific information on marine mammal use of Howland.
Within 10 years of CCP approval, increase scientific understanding of marine mammal presence and use of Howland marine waters. The desired conditions by which this will be met will be to document all marine mammal use of nearshore waters.
Strategies Applied to Achieve Objective
Incidental observations of marine mammals.
Solicit partnership for study of marine mammals at Howland.
Rationale:
NOAA, the Service, Oceanic Institute, University of Hawaii, and Bishop Museum marine biologists have collected data on marine species of concern since 2000. Only anecdotal information exists on marine mammal use of the waters surrounding Howland Island. However, studies elsewhere in the Pacific indicate that waters surrounding small islands may support distinct local populations of marine mammals. It is also important to understand the threats human activity may pose to this important resource (Marine Mammal Commission. pers. comm.), including unauthorized fishing.

Goal 4: Protect, maintain, enhance, and preserve the wilderness character of Howland's terrestrial and marine communities.

Objective 4a: Protect and maintain wilderness values.
Upon CCP approval, continue to preserve the wilderness values (e.g. size, naturalness, solitude, supplemental values) of Howland. Achievement of this objective will be evaluated by assessing loss or degradation of values that qualified it for potential designation (see Appendix F).
Strategies Applied to Achieve Objective
Use minimum tools necessary to manage refuge resources.
Continue to manage Howland as wilderness.
Monitor values of naturalness and solitude.
Rationale:
Howland has been and is managed as a wild, natural area due to its remote location, historic lack of human impact, and limited human presence. Areas of Howland have been identified as meeting the criteria for a Wilderness Study Area (Appendix F). Completion of the wilderness review process and as appropriate development of a Legislative EIS will be pursued for all Pacific Remote Island Refuges once their CCP's have been completed.

Some human generated debris remains from past occupations. Additionally, debris such as discarded fishing nets continuously washes ashore. This debris impinges upon wilderness values.

In the interim, all areas identified as suitable WSAs would continue to be managed as wilderness. All management activities would be conducted in such a manner as not to detract from the wilderness values identified in the Wilderness Inventory.

Goal 5: Howland's biological, cultural and historic resources are preserved.

Objective 5a: Protect cultural resources.
Upon CCP approval, continue to protect existing cultural resources. The desired conditions by which this will be met will be to document any change in condition of Amelia Earhart day beacon memorial, or other recognized cultural/historical resource.
Strategy Applied to Achieve Objective
Record incidental observations of condition of cultural resources.
Rationale:
Restricting human use of Howland would maintain cultural resources by limiting the opportunity for invasive species establishment, and reducing the opportunity for unauthorized collection or disturbance. In order to keep cultural resource sites protected, the locations and descriptions of fragile cultural resources would not be made available to the public.

Objective 5b: Enhance Law Enforcement Capabilities
Upon CCP approval, seek to improve partnerships with the NOAA Office of Law Enforcement to increase enforcement capacity. The desired conditions by which this will be met will be to formalize interagency agreements and develop remote surveillance techniques to document unauthorized access to the refuge.
Strategies Applied to Achieve Objective
Establish joint enforcement operational protocols with NOAA Office of Law enforcement.
Evaluate the effectiveness of deploying acoustical devices to detect ship traffic in the vicinity of the refuge.
Rationale:
Enhancing law enforcement capability to detect and prosecute unauthorized access would preserve biological and cultural resources by limiting the opportunity for invasive species establishment and deterring unauthorized collection or disturbance.

Goal 6: An informed, interested, and educated public appreciates remote Pacific Island NWR wilderness values, cultural and historical resources, and their ecosystems, with special emphasis on seabirds.

Objective 6a: Provide off-site education and interpretation opportunities.
Within three years of CCP approval, develop an off-site educational opportunity for the public to learn about Pacific Island refuge wilderness values, cultural and historical resources, tropical island ecosystems, seabirds, and coral reef. The desired conditions by which this will be met will be through publications, educational programs, displays, or other media.
Strategy Applied to Achieve Objective
Develop, with External Affairs office, Honolulu, an interpretative brochure, display, or educational program for all remote Pacific Island refuges.
Rationale:
While it is important for the public to understand and appreciate the resource values associated with remote island refuges, it is logistically difficult to do this on-site at Howland and still protect the island's wildlife, habitats, wilderness values, cultural and historical resources, and visitor's safety. For these reasons, interpretative or educational opportunities for the public to learn and appreciate the values of remote Pacific Island refuges and resources will be provided primarily as off-site programs and interpretative brochures.

Chapter 4: REFUGE AND RESOURCE DESCRIPTION

Geographic/Ecosystem Setting

Howland Island, located at approximately lat. 0°49' N. and long. 176°38' W is a northwestern outlier of the Phoenix Archipelago and is included in the Central Pacific subregion of the Polynesian Region of the Pacific Basin. This subregion, the largest of four in the Polynesian Region, is the most remote part of the tropical Pacific and includes only low-lying reef islands, atolls, and submerged reefs. Vegetation patterns are determined by the highly variable but normally low rainfall levels found along the Equator in the central Pacific. In turn, the arid weather and ocean circulation patterns impose limits on floating seed plant dispersal strategies. Howland falls in the central Pacific dry zone with rainfall less than 40 inches per year, and thus "cannot support any forest or closed woody vegetation" (Mueller-Dombois and Fosberg 1998). The nearest landmasses are Baker Island 32 nmi to the south, and McKean Island 352 nmi to the south southeast. Both islands are also in the Phoenix Islands. The remaining 8 Phoenix Islands under the jurisdiction of the Republic of Kiribati are the next closest neighbors to Howland Island, up to 480 nmi to the southeast. The next closest landmasses outside the Phoenix Islands are the Gilbert Islands, with Beru Island closest to Howland Island at 420 nmi to the southwest. Tarawa Atoll, the capitol of the Republic of Kiribati, is 600 nmi to the west in the central Gilbert Archipelago.

Climate

General Climate and Related Oceanographic Conditions in the Central Equatorial Pacific

The climate associated with Howland Island can be generalized as being arid, warm, and tropical with moderate breezes and light to moderate rainfall. Although differences in climate exist among the islands, climate monitoring stations are not readily available in the equatorial Pacific. Consequently, site-specific data is lacking for most central Pacific locations, or have only been collected for a short period. In order to describe the weather conditions on Howland Island, weather monitoring data are taken from historic onsite weather data, or from the closest weather monitoring station, located on Kanton Island.

There are several climatic factors that influence weather on Howland: trade winds, rainfall, and oceanic currents. Trade winds are surface winds that typically dominate airflow in tropical regions and predominate from the southeast at Howland between 12-17 miles per hour. Atmospheric pressure gradients range from high pressure areas located near lat. 30° N. and lat. 30° S., to the low pressure band located near lat. 5° N., driving both the northeast and southeast trade winds. This area of low pressure located just north of the Equator is referred to as the 'doldrums' or the Intertropical Convergence Zone (ITCZ) and lacks these prevailing trade winds because they converge and rise upward.

Solar heating also allows the moist air mass of the ITCZ to rise, thus cooling the air mass and producing a band of heavy precipitation several degrees to either side of the ITCZ (Wallace and Hobbs 1977). Howland's position near the Equator places it outside this band of heavy precipitation. Changes in these typical patterns occur seasonally and during periodic events known as the El Niño Southern Oscillation (ENSO). During an ENSO event, the ITCZ shifts south and east toward unusually warmer waters. At Howland, this shift typically leads to lighter wind speeds and more rainfall (USFWS 2001, USFWS 1998a, Vitousek et al. 1980).

Prevailing ocean currents surrounding Howland Island also influence weather patterns on the island by moderating the surrounding surface air temperatures. These surface currents roughly mimic the direction of the trade winds. Howland is almost always within the flow regime of the westward flowing South Equatorial Current.

Howland Island also lies in the path of the subsurface easterly flowing Equatorial Undercurrent (EUC) also referred to as the Cromwell Current. As the EUC strikes the submerged western slopes of Howland Island, nutrient rich waters are deflected upward, enriching the primary productivity of the surface waters surrounding Howland. These upwelling waters from the EUC are slightly cooler than adjacent sea surface waters and may moderate the effects of localized and periodic sea surface warming events.

Howland Island Climate Data

There is very little weather data available from Howland Island. Weather observations were made during the military occupation of Baker and Howland Islands from 1935-1945 (AEC 1963). However, these military records could not be located within refuge files in Honolulu. A single reconnaissance trip to Howland and Baker Islands by the Logistics Planning Group of Holmes & Narver INC, for the U.S. Atomic Energy Commission (AEC) in October 1963 recorded sea water temperatures between 86°F and 87°F (AEC 1963). Air temperatures during that time period ranged from 80°F to 94°F with an average of 85°F. Wind speeds during this visit averaged 13 miles per hour with a range of 6-23 miles per hour. In winter, the average daily range of air temperature is reported as 78-88°F, and during summer the average daily range is 78-90°F (NOAA 1991).

The nearest weather station to Howland is at Kanton Atoll, located in the Phoenix Islands at lat. 02°46' S., long. 171°43' W., or roughly 378 nmi southeast of Howland (USFWS 1998a). This station reports total annual rainfall is approximately 30 inches with precipitation consistent throughout the year (NOAA 1991). Weather data at Kanton support the conclusions of arid conditions in the northern Phoenix Islands.

Global Climate Change

A continuously growing body of unequivocal scientific evidence has emerged supporting the anthropogenic nature of current global climate change. During the 20th century, the global environment experienced variations in average worldwide temperatures, sea levels, and chemical concentrations. Global air temperatures on the earth's surface have increased by 1.3°F since the mid-19th century (IPCC. 2007a). Eleven of 12 years from 1995 to 2006 are the warmest on record since 1850 (IPCC 2007b). Global water temperatures have increased by 0.31° on average in the upper 300 m during the past 60 years since 1948 and changes in ocean heat content have penetrated as deep as 3000 meters (Levitus et al. 2005). Subsequently, sea levels rose approximately 1.7 mm (0.07 in) ± 0.5 mm/yr during the 20th century (IPCC. 2007a); this rate rose dramatically to 3.1 mm (0.122 in) ± 0.7mm/yr since 1993 (IPCC 2007b).

While the concept of climate change is now widely accepted, the extent and impact of future changes as well as the exact source (natural or human induced) remains a debate (OPIC 2000). Emerging consensus contends that increasing quantities of greenhouse gases (GHGs) in the atmosphere, especially carbon dioxide (CO_2), are beginning to affect climate and may be the dominant force driving recent warming trends. The amount of GHGs globally has grown due to human activities since pre-industrial times, with an increase of 70% between 1970 and 2004 (IPCC 2007b). Carbon dioxide has increased by about 80% in the same time period. The atmospheric concentrations of CO_2 and methane in 2005 were 379 ppm³ and 1774 ppb, respectively. These amounts greatly exceed concentrations recorded in the global environment over the last 650,000 years (IPCC, 2007a). Other emissions and GHGs from human activity have enhanced the heat trapping capability of the earth's atmosphere, causing warmer temperatures. Although the increase in carbon dioxide is largely attributed to fossil fuel use, land use changes have also increased the amount of cleared land surfaces, thereby reflecting more solar radiation (IPCC 2001, IPCC 2007a, IPCC, 2007b).

Global forecasting models offer a variety of predictions based on different emission scenarios. OPIC (2000) suggests that a further increase in GHG emissions could double atmospheric concentrations of CO_2 by 2060 and subsequently increase temperatures by as much as 2 to 6.5°F over the next century. Recent model experiments by the IPCC (2007a) show that if GHGs and other emissions remain at 2000 levels, a further global average temperature warming of about 0.18°F per decade is expected. Sea-level rise is expected to accelerate by two to five times the current rates due to both ocean thermal expansion and the melting of glaciers and polar ice caps. Consequently, patterns of precipitation and evaporation may be altered. These changes may lead to more severe weather, shifts in ocean circulation (currents, upwelling), as well as adverse impacts to economies and human health (OPIC 2000, IPCC 2001, Buddemeier et al. 2004, IPCC 2007a). Hansen, et al. (2008) propose that current models may underestimate the slower feedback processes such as ice sheet disintegration, vegetation migration, and greenhouse gas release from soils and that these factors may come into play in this century. These changes will have a significant effect on the national wildlife refuges in the tropical Pacific. The changing global environment and the implications this may have for ecological and geological processes in the Central Tropical Pacific are important considerations for future management of trust resources there. The four areas of impact linked to global climate change that may have the greatest potential effect on Howland Island NWR and its wildlife are sea level rise, weather and ocean circulation changes, ecological disruptions and coral bleaching due to increased ocean temperature, and oceanic chemical composition change.

Vitousek (1994) reported, "Changes in both climate and biological diversity are known with less certainty than are changes in CO_2 concentrations, global biogeochemistry or land use." Because temperature is more variable both spatially and temporally than CO_2 concentration, it is difficult to separate human-caused vs. natural background variation. However, it is certain that increasing concentrations of CO_2 and other greenhouse gasses will cause increasing climate change (Vitousek, 1994).

The equatorial locale for Howland places it near the path of anomalous water current and surface wind conditions during ENSO events, but the paucity of weather and oceanographic data at Howland renders it difficult to assess the impacts and trends of global climate change at the island. The upward deflection of cool subsurface waters into shallow water by the upwelling effects of the EUC further complicates an assessment of climate change effects, because this phenomenon has been rarely reported outside of the three equatorial refuges (Howland, Baker, Jarvis).

The insular nature of both the terrestrial and coral reef habitats of Howland will result in the same high vulnerability of resident organisms that is seen in range restricted or mountaintop species elsewhere (Parmesan 2006).

Sea Level Rise

While global temperature is projected to rise by 3.6 to 9°F and sea level to rise by more than 31.5 inches during the next two centuries, sea levels have fluctuated by an order of 328 feet over the past 18,000 years as natural background variation and thawing out from the last ice age (Michener et al. 1997). Contributions to sea level rise by climate change are ice-sheet melting, alpine glacier melting and thermal expansion of the sea. Sea levels have risen by 4-8 inches during the past century (Michener et al. 1997). The Intergovernmental Panel on Climate Change (IPCC 2001) predicted a sea level rise of 3.5 inches to 34.6 inches by the year 2100 unless greenhouse gas emissions were reduced substantially. They also suggested that continuing greenhouse gas emissions could trigger polar ice-cap melting after 2100 accompanied by sea level rise greater than 16 feet. More recent modeling indicates that melting could occur faster than the IPCC predicted (Overpeck et al. 2006).

Evidence also suggests that the world's oceans are regionally divisible with regard to historic fluctuations in sea level. Localized variations in subsidence and emergence of the sea floor and plate-tectonics activity prevent extrapolations in sea level fluctuations and trends between different regions. While researchers in IPCC (2007a) state that water levels in the equatorial Pacific are rising at a rate of 1.2 to 2 mm per year, it may not be possible to discuss uniform changes in sea level on a global scale, or the magnitude of greenhouse gas-forced changes, as these changes may vary regionally (Michener et al. 1997). As an example, tide gauge records on the Atlantic coast indicate a sea level rise of 0.06 to 0.16 in/year over the past century, whereas, they have indicated a 0.35 to 0.39 in/year increase along the Gulf Coast of the United States (Michener et al. 1997).

Increases in sea level and associated increases in storm surges and storm intensity will affect Howland Island. Shoreline erosion and salt water intrusion into subsurface freshwater aquifers have been noted throughout the Pacific (Shea et al. 2001). Due to the deep marine slopes directly adjacent to Howland Island, increases in sea level could significantly erode shorelines and overall island surface area since opportunities for accretion of lands do not exist. Loss of breeding habitat for seabirds, wintering grounds for migratory shorebirds, and habitat for native plants, and land crabs are predicted at current rates of sea level rise.

Ocean Temperature Increases

Most climate projections suggest that more intense wind speeds and precipitation amounts will accompany more frequent tropical typhoon/cyclones and increased tropical-sea surface temperatures in the next 50 years (Walther et al. 2002, IPCC, 2007). The third IPCC (2001) has concluded, with "moderate confidence" that the intensity of tropical cyclones is likely to increase by 10-20 percent in the Pacific region when atmospheric levels of CO_2 reach double pre-industrial levels (IPCC 2001). One model projects a doubling of the frequency of 4-inch-per-day rainfall events and a 15–18 percent increase in rainfall intensity over large areas of the Pacific (IPCC 2001). The IPCCl (2007) states that it is "more likely than not" that the rise in intense tropical cyclones is due to anthropogenic activity.

Above normal mean sea surface temperatures have been shown to cause bleaching and mortality in corals both in nature and in the laboratory with bleaching generally occurring in shallower waters (Floros et al. 2004). Coral bleaching, the expulsion of symbiotic zooxanthellae from coral polyps and subsequent loss of photosynthetic pigments is the result of both natural and anthropogenic stresses. Although corals may pale in response to seasonal increases in sea surface temperature, there has been a higher frequency of large scale bleaching events since the 1980s (Nicholls et al. 2007). The most severe global bleaching event ever recorded occurred in 1997-98 when over 50 countries showed signs of bleaching (Grimsditch and Salm 2005). Many species of coral currently exist in the upper limits of their specific temperature range; thus, an increase in average sea surface temperatures (even by 1.8 or 3.6°F) over a sustained period has been shown to cause mass bleaching, especially in shallow waters habitats (Grimsditch and Salm 2005). Other variables have also been implicated in bleaching and mortality events, including, extended periods of high temperatures, low wind velocity, clear skies, calm seas, low rainfall, high rainfall, salinity changes, high turbidity or acute pollution. Floros et al. (2004) goes on to note "The causes of coral bleaching are debatable, but widely thought to be the result of a variety of stresses, both natural and human-induced, that cause the degeneration and the loss of the colored zooxanthellae from the coral tissues."

Bleaching episodes in equatorial islands appear to be linked to the El Niño-Southern Oscillation (ENSO). Widespread bleaching events occurred during the El Niños of 1982-83, 1987-88, and 1997-98 (Buddemeier et al. 2004). During the warm phase of ENSO, or El Niño, sea-surface temperatures are usually warm, trade winds weak, and sea level decreases in the western Pacific (IPCC 2001, Buddemeier et al. 2004). These combined factors result in a dramatic increase in coral bleaching (Buddemeier et al. 2004). While El Niño events have increased in intensity and frequency over the past decades, some longer-term records have not found a direct link to global warming (Cobb et al. 2003) and do not predict significant changes in El Niño; however, they do suggest an evolution toward more "El Niño-like" patterns (Buddemeier et al. 2004). Most climate projections reveal that this trend is likely to increase rapidly in the next 50 years (Walther et al. 2002).

Most climate projections suggest that more intense wind speeds and precipitation amounts will accompany more frequent tropical typhoon/cyclones and increased tropical-sea surface temperatures in the next 50 years (Walther et al. 2002, IPCC. 2007a). The third IPCC (2001) has concluded, with "moderate confidence" that the intensity of tropical cyclones is likely to increase by 10 to 20 percent in the Pacific region when atmospheric levels of CO_2 reach double pre-industrial levels (IPCC 2001). One model projects a doubling of the frequency of 4 inches per day rainfall events and a 15-18 percent increase in rainfall intensity over large areas of the Pacific (IPCC 2001). The IPCC (2007a) states that it is "more likely than not" that the rise in intense tropical cyclones is due to anthropogenic activity.

If coral reef ecosystems do not acclimate to projected thermal stresses, more frequent bleaching events and widespread mortality will occur. The ability of coral reef ecosystems to withstand these impacts will depend on the extent of degradation from other anthropogenic pressures and the frequency of future bleaching events (Nicholls et al. 2007).

Field observation of corals at Baker, Howland, and Jarvis during five separate expeditions from 2000-2006 indicate that corals may be recovering from a bleaching event that took place during the previous few years (1997-1998). Corals continued to increase in cover and size based upon observations during all subsequent (post 2000) visits, including those at permanent transect sites (Maragos 2008; Maragos et al. 2008a & 2008b, Miller et al. 2008). Although coral bleaching was predicted to occur at Jarvis in 2003 based upon NOAA satellite based temperature and wind data, no evidence of bleaching was reported there during the early 2004 and 2006 visits (Maragos 2000-2006, unpublished data). One possible explanation is that the cool upwelling waters of the EUC are buffering the effects of the otherwise warmer seawater temperatures at the island.

Tudhope (2000) sampled 6 cores obtained from 2 large, 3-4 meter *Porites* coral heads at Jarvis in 1999 to track sea surface temperature and coral growth rates over several or more decades using stable oxygen isotope as a measure of Sea Surface Temperature. He found a good correlation between this measure and the NINO3.4 Index, which is one of the most widely used and reliable indicators of the status of ENSO. The results of their work at Jarvis and at four other tropical sites in the Line and Cook Islands contributed to demonstrating linkages between the tropics and the North Pacific over hundreds of years (D'arrigo et al 2005). Hawaii Undersea Research Laboratory (HURL) submersible dives at Jarvis in July 2005 revealed many deep-water corals, and samples of some were taken for climate change and paleo-climate analyses. The results of these analyses are not yet available.

Oceanic Acidification and Atmospheric Chemistry

Glacial and interglacial periods in the Earth's history, as measured from deep Antarctic ice cores, reveal cyclical fluctuations in the concentration of global CO_2. However, recent increases fall outside the range of peak prehistoric CO_2 levels. Current atmospheric CO_2 concentrations are at their highest levels in more than 160,000 years, with humans emitting 25 billion tons of CO_2 annually (Buddemeier et al. 2004). The rate of increase is also five to ten times more rapid than any of the sustained changes in the ice-core record (Vitousek 1994). The higher the concentration of CO_2 in the atmosphere, the greater the amount of CO_2 dissolved in the surface ocean. When CO_2 dissolves in seawater it forms carbonic acid (H_2CO_3), a weak acid that releases additional hydrogen ions and increases the acidity of the ocean. In order to buffer this acidity, the hydrogen ions react with carbonate (CO_3^{2-}) ions and convert them to bicarbonate ions (HCO_3^-). However, this buffering ability has diminished due to the rapid rising CO_2 concentrations and the global seawater pH has decreased by 0.1 units since 1750, with regional variations (Royal Society 2005, IPCC 2007). Models predict that over the 21st century, average surface ocean pH will continue to fall between 0.14 and 0.35 units (IPCC 2007a).

Increased atmospheric CO_2 and ocean acidification affect marine organisms. As the concentration of carbonic acid and bicarbonate ions rises, the concentration of carbonate ions decreases. Many corals and marine organisms use calcium (Ca^{2+}) and carbonate ions from seawater to secrete $CaCO_3$ skeletons (Buddemeier et al. 2004, IPCC 2007). Change in CO_2 levels will increase the partial pressure of CO_2 in seawater, thus reducing the over-saturation of aragonite, a form of calcium carbonate that is the major building block for coral reefs (Vitousek, 1994). On a transect in the Pacific Ocean that ran very near Jarvis, Feeley et al. (2004) show that the aragonite saturation horizon is shallow and is shoaling compared to the pre-industrial aragonite saturation horizon. This reduces the width of the zone in which marine organisms have optimum aragonite concentrations for shell-building. The result of this is uncertain but is thought to reduce the rate at which corals can deposit calcium carbonate, thus reducing the rate at which coral reefs will be able to keep up with any increases in sea level. A lowered calcification rate means calcifying organisms (corals) may grow skeletons at a slower rate, lower density, and/or decreasing strength. Thus, changes in global seawater chemistry reduce the ability of corals to successfully compete for space and increase susceptibility to breakage (Grimsditch and Salm 2005). In addition to changes in the carbonate system, changes in ocean chemistry may affect the availability of nutrients and toxins to marine organisms.

It should also be noted that chemical composition changes in the atmosphere may also affect terrestrial ecosystems. For instance, the quantity of nitrogen available to organisms affects species composition and productivity. Increase in nitrogen can alter species composition by favoring those plant species that respond to nitrogen increases (Vitousek, 1994). Increased carbon dioxide can also affect photosynthetic rates in plants, change levels and characteristics of secondary compounds in plant tissues, change plant species composition, lower nutrient levels, and lower weight gain by herbivores.

Geology and Soils

Howland Island is a low-lying, nearly level island with a slightly depressed central area surrounded by a narrow shallow fringing reef. The submarine slopes descend steeply to great depths beyond the fringing reefs (Maragos et al. 2008a). Surface deposits on the island consist of calcareous sands and coral rock. Soil texture is coarse and not easily compacted. The central depression is likely the result of the combined effects of guano mining more than a century ago and wave action depositing sand rocks and boulders around the island's fringe. The island was likely formed as a result of submarine volcanic activity and changes in the earth's crust caused by continental tectonic plate movement, including emergence of a high volcanic island, its later subsidence, reef accretion, and its gradual northwesterly drift away from the East Pacific Rise over the past 50 to 80 million years. Although scientists since Darwin (1842) have been pondering seamount, island, and atoll formation in the Pacific, the specifics of how Howland Island was formed have not been investigated, although they would likely follow the general sequence first postulated by Darwin.

The dominant theory of atoll formation states that islands form in deep tropical oceans as a result of underwater volcanoes that grow to the surface to form high volcanic islands, giving coral polyps a foundation to grow upon and form reefs fringing the island. In the Pacific most of these volcanoes originated at the East Pacific Rise or at hotspots (Maragos et al. 2008a). In time, the volcano becomes dormant, and its mass pushes down on the earth's crust causing it and its island to subside and shrink in size, while its fringing reefs continue to grow upward and maintain proximity to the sea surface. Coral reefs, originally fringing the edges of a large island, may become barrier reefs around larger islands outlining the contour of the original coastline, with a lagoon occupying the space vacated by the shrinking island. Eventually, further subsidence causes the island to disappear completely from the lagoon leaving behind an atoll. However, for small islands such as Howland, lagoons may not have formed at latter stages, and continued subsidence has left only a small low reef island in its wake. Based upon deep drilling through the atolls in the Marshall Islands in the 1940s and 1950s, it is believed that these processes occurred well before the beginning of the last ice age (approximately 115,000 years ago) and encompassed more than 50 to 60 million years and up to several thousand feet of reef growth equal to the degree of subsidence over that time span. In addition, it is hypothesized that changes in sea level associated with the end of the last ice age and the deposition of highly permeable coralline limestone (calcium carbonate) derived from the remains of marine organisms likely contributed to the carbonate platform that characterizes the contemporary geologic structure of Howland Island.

The entire western or leeward beach of the island is sandy and low, while the eastern side, constantly pounded by waves generated by the trade winds, is higher, more abrupt, and covered with coral rubble and sandstone slabs. There is no pronounced beach crest or central basin (dry lagoon) typically found on some larger low-lying reef islands. Soils of low-lying atolls in the Pacific frequently consist of accumulations organic matter, guano, pumice, or other transported material on top of a calcareous sand or limestone substratum (Morrison 1990). The soil of Howland Island is composed of coral fragments and light brown coral sand with a low percentage of organic matter.

Hutchinson (1950) concluded that phosphates accumulate preferentially on islands, such as Howland, Baker, and Jarvis, that are situated in climatic dry belts used by large populations of seabirds. Deposits of phosphate-rich soils have formed over time from guano deposited on the island by fish-eating seabirds. Mild acids formed from the decomposition of organic matter carry the guano downward in the soil to limestone soil layers where acids are neutralized and calcium phosphate is accumulating from the chemical changes. In addition, when guano-beds are exposed to rain their soluble constituents are removed and the insoluble matter is left behind. The soluble phosphates washed out of the guano may also become fixed to the coral sand and limestone by the process described above. The calcium phosphate rocks and soil occur among the sedimentary strata and were the principal sources of phosphate targeted for commercial fertilizer use during the guano mining period between 1861 and 1891 (see Chapter 3.15). Even after the guano mining era, the soil profile still contained heavy guano deposits (Christophersen 1927).

Hydrology

No information is available on the subsurface hydrology of Howland Island. However, its small size and prevailing arid rainfall conditions would not likely result in the formation of a drinkable groundwater lens. During staff visits to Howland, potable water is carried in containers to the island for short staff visits, and could be produced on site via reverse osmosis technology for prolonged staff visits, just as it is now produced for permanent field stations at other remote Pacific Island NWRs.

Air and Water Quality

Due to the lack of human presence, oceanic and air quality are expected to be good and lacking in pollutants. Vapors from abandoned spilled fuel storage drums left behind during the World War II era are likely to be confined to the immediate vicinity of the drums and have probably all volatized. The acoustic environment at Howland is completely natural without any anthropogenic noise except during periodic staff visits. On the island, dominant natural sounds include the wind, calls of seabird and shorebirds, and seawater lapping on the shoreline with wave action crashing further offshore on the outer reef margin. Underwater the dominant sounds are wave action and surge striking the reef slopes and the sounds of thousands of feeding and moving invertebrates and fish.

Environmental Contaminants

Fuel storage drums left behind by the U.S. military during the World War II era contained residual aviation and motor fuel. In 1987, the U.S. Army Corps of Engineers, sponsored by funds from the Defense Environmental Restoration Program, organized an expedition to Howland and Baker to dispose of the fuel by burning it on-site while in the drums (H. Takemoto, per. comm.). However, the Corps efforts did not completely consume the fuel, and the burning left toxic residues in many of the drums and surrounding soils (Lee Ann Woodward, USFWS, per. comm.). At Howland Island, there were only a handful of these drums. The total area affected by the drums and contaminated soil is estimated at 26 yd^2. The main source of contamination is rusting steel and iron from various machine parts and drums.

Terrestrial Vegetation and Habitats

Howland Island is vegetated with grasses, herbaceous plants, and shrubs. Areas devoid of vegetation occur along exposed beach and shoreline areas. Only strand species able to survive long periods of drought and irregular opportunities to reproduce during the infrequent wet years of the ENSO persist here. By 1924 when Christophersen (1927) did the first thorough survey of Howland Island's vegetation, there had already been approximately a century of visits by Europeans and guano miners. Despite this traffic and the potential for introductions, Christophersen found a very depauperate flora consisting of five native species (*Lepturus repens, Boerhavia* sp., *Portulaca lutea, Tribulus cistoides, and Cordia subcordata*) and one that had probably been accidentally introduced (*Portulaca oleracea*). Since then at least 4 more species were intentionally introduced (*Cocos nucifera, Casuarina* sp., *Pandanus* sp., and *Coccoloba uvifera*) and at least 7 as wave carried adventives or additional accidental introductions by humans *(Digitaria pacifica, Sophora tomentosa, Sida fallax, Scaevola taccada, Suriana maritima*, and *Tournefortia argentea)* for a contemporary total of only 16 species (see Appendix B). On a short visit in 2004, only nine species of plants were located (Flint and Eggleston 2004). It is likely that seeds of additional species are regularly washing up on the beach and then dying back as conditions become too dry or high surf washes the plants away. Table B-3, Appendix B, lists all the plant species of Howland Island, collections or first observations, and most recent information about current presence or absence.

The structure of the plant community is grassland and low forbs cover. A single grove of kou (*Cordia subcordata*) in shrub growth form reaching 15 feet high grows in the interior. The kou along with tree heliotrope (*Tournefortia*) and naupaka (*Scaevola*) bordering the beach serve as important nesting and roosting habitat for the red-footed booby and cover for wintering bristle-thighed curlews. Great frigatebirds and white terns also prefer to nest above the ground on the few shrubs available, but all the other species nest directly on the ground. Shrubs and rock piles also provide shade and daytime cover for the numerous land hermit crabs, *Coenobita perlatus* that inhabit Howland Island.

Terrestrial Wildlife

Seabirds, shorebirds, lizards, vegetation, insects, crabs, and invasive rats and feral cats have been observed and studied at Howland Island during the current century. The Service subsequently eradicated all rats and cats from the island to allow repopulation by several nesting seabird species and greater use by all remaining indigenous terrestrial species.

Seabirds and Land Mammals

There are no native land mammals at Howland Island. Numerically dominant vertebrates are migratory seabirds and shorebirds. Howland Island falls into the North American Bird Conservation Region (BCR) 68 along with all the other island territories of the United States. Earliest ornithological surveys at Howland Island took place long after the introduction of the Polynesian rat (*Rattus exulans*) so the composition of the avian community prior to human contact can only be surmised by looking at other islands in the Phoenix Archipelago that did not suffer the invasion of rats. The findings of the ornithologist on the Whippoorwill Expedition of 1924 are the only comprehensive ornithological records prior to 1963, when scientists from the Smithsonian Institution visited eight times between 1963 and 1965. Table B-4 in Appendix B lists species and estimates of numbers for seabird species on all staff visits since 1973. Munro (1924) found 11 species of seabirds breeding in 1924.

Several avian species are listed by various authorities as species of concern. Of note, seabird species listed by IUCN as Vulnerable include Phoenix petrel (*Pterodroma alba*) and the Polynesian storm-petrel (*Nesofregetta fuliginosa*), both of which probably occurred at Howland Island prior to the introduction of rats. The Phoenix petrel is also considered a bird of National Conservation Concern by the Service and the Phoenix petrel and Polynesian storm-petrel are classified as highly imperiled in the Pacific Region Seabird Conservation plan. The blue noddy (*Procelsterna cerulean*) and lesser frigatebird (*Fregata ariel*) are included in the category of High concern in that document (USFWS 2005).

Cats were introduced during 1935 to 1942 resulting in decreased abundance and diversity of seabirds species breeding at Howland by 1963 (Sibley et al., 1965). After feral cats were removed in 1986, 11 seabird species are again breeding and 2 Procellariform species (Wedge-tailed Shearwaters *Puffinus pacificus* and an unidentified storm-petrel) that likely bred there prior to rat introduction have been seen on the ground in the colony presaging re-colonization. The three most numerous breeding species at Howland are the lesser frigatebird (*Fregata ariel*) [a BCC or bird of conservation concern in BCR (Bird Conservation Region) 68 and listed as a bird of High concern at the Regional level], masked booby, (*Sula dactylatra*), and sooty tern (*Onychoprion fuscatus*). Table B-4 also provides the breeding seabird species at Howland.

Shorebirds

Species occurrence and counts of the eight migratory shorebird species recorded from Howland Island are displayed in Table B-4, Appendix B. The four most common migrants wintering at Howland are ruddy turnstone (*Arenaria interpres*), Pacific golden plover (*Pluvialis fulva*), bristle-thighed curlew (*Numenius tahitiensis*), and wandering tattler (*Heteroscelus incanus*). Of these, the bristle-thighed curlew and the Pacific golden plover are considered species of High Concern in the national conservation priority scheme for shorebirds (Engilis and Naughton 2004). All of the species mentioned above except wandering tattler are labeled as high concern in the Regional shorebird plan and Bristle–thighed Curlews and Pacific Golden Plovers are Birds of Conservation Concern in BCR 68. These islands provide crucial wintering habitat and may serve as rest-stops for arctic-breeding shorebirds wintering farther south in the Pacific Islands.

Reptiles

Only two species of terrestrial reptiles have been reported from Howland Island: snake-eyed skink (*Cryptoblepharus peocidopleurus*) and mourning gecko (*Lipidodactylus lugubris*). Both species were first reported by Hague in 1862, and served as alternate prey for cats when they were present on Howland Island. Only the snake-eyed skink has been observed during recent visits to Howland.

Invertebrates (crabs and insects)

Howland Island is home to a large number of the land crab, *Coenobita perlata*. Their large biomass plays a dominant role in terrestrial food webs on the island where they consume a wide variety of organic matter of all types. Other terrestrial arthropods and mollusks are very poorly known. The entomologist Edward L. Caum visited Howland Island in 1924 and a number of other naturalists collected insects on subsequent trips but there are no published accounts or lists until Ashley Browne of the University of Hawaii visited in 1939 and published a short note listing 3 species of insects that were collected (Browne 1940). Recent observations, but not collections, during staff visits by Service biologists include house flies, small ants, moths, millers, butterflies, and spiders.

Kirkpatric and Rauzon (1986) compared food habits of feral cats at Howland and Jarvis Islands. Although there were crickets, cockroaches and tenebrionid beetles in the stomach of Jarvis cats (n=73), no insect remains were found in a smaller sample (n=5) of Howland Island cats.

Marine Habitats, Fish, and Wildlife

Previous Surveys

Before regular marine assessment and monitoring efforts began in 2000, marine scientists visited Howland to collect fish, corals, and perhaps other reef life, but there were no systematic surveys of the reefs in the literature. Extensive collections of reef fishes were accomplished by Fowler (1927), anon. (1950), Helfrich (1962), and Wass (1966). More recently, the Smithsonian Institution Pacific Ocean Biological Survey (SIPOBS), and others in Mundy et al (2002) continued this work. The dominant reef life studied during post-1997 expeditions include: benthic algae (Peter Vroom, Kim Paige per. comm.), corals and anemones (John Schmerfeld, Jim Maragos, Greta Aeby and Jean Kenyon per. comm.), other reef invertebrates (Scott Godwin, Dwayne Minton, and Robin Newbold per. comm.), and reef fishes (Ed DeMartini, Bruce Mundy, Brian Zgliczynski, Brian Green, Richard Wass, Alan Friedlander, Stephanie Holzwarth, and others per. comm.).

Five sets of recent surveys through early 2006, have been accomplished in cooperation with the NOAA Pacific Islands Fisheries Science Center (PIFSC) and their research vessels (*Townsend Cromwell, Oscar Elton Sette,* and *Hi'ialakai*), primarily through the sponsorship of the Center's Coral Reef Ecosystem Division (CRED) (R. Brainard, per. comm.). The surveys since 2000, are of several types including oceanographic data collection, towed diver surveys, rapid ecological assessments (REA) at stationary sites, and collections of marine animals and plants for identification and description in the lab. The Service, with assistance from CRED established three permanently marked transects to document trends in corals and some macro-invertebrates over time since 2000.

Despite these intense efforts, several important habitats at Howland have not been adequately surveyed. Shallow reef terraces off both the southern and northern horns of the island are bathed in strong, turbulent and at times unpredictable currents, preventing REAs at both ends. In addition, the windward reefs were inaccessible during most staff visits because of heavy tradewind generated waves close to the reef and onshore winds that would push the dive skiffs too close to the reefs. Moreover, due to safety concerns, dives have generally been limited to depths of 65 feet and one hour duration. Because of these limitations, some important habitats are still poorly sampled and deep slope habitats (164 to 3,281 ft) within the refuge remain mostly unexplored, except for early 2006 acquisition of high resolution bathymetry of Howland from Multi-Beam™ surveys (S. Ferguson, per. comm.) and substantial oceanographic data (R. Brainard, per. comm.).

At the time of this CCP, data from coral, other marine invertebrates, algae, and fish surveys were available for review and compilation, and Maragos et al. (2008a) and Miller et al. (2008) provide updated compilations based upon site visits through 2006.

Submergent Habitats

Howland's shallow marine benthic habitats consist of fringing reef crests, shallow back reefs, steep fore reefs, spurs-and-grooves, and small reef terraces. The last two habitats are restricted to the windward (east side) of the island. In addition, a shallow short channel was blasted through the narrow fringing reef during the pre-World War II era to facilitate small boat access between the shoreline and ocean. The deep slope habitats below depths of 65-98 feet have not been surveyed by divers, although remotely operated vehicles (ROVs) have been launched to collect video- and camera-based data. Pelagic habitats occur further offshore beyond the influence of upwelling and nearshore oceanographic processes. Nearshore habitats include distinct upwelling zones off the west side of the island; oligotrophic waters off the windward reefs; and turbulent rip currents and possibly mesoscale eddies off the north and south ends of the island. The PIFSC has conducted oceanographic research off the island to contrast the differences between nutrient rich upwelling zones and the ambient nutrient-poor ocean conditions outside areas of upwelling currents.

Reef Life

The marine ecosystem of Howland remains mostly undisturbed and pristine. Multitudes of marine species inhabit and visit the shallow water habitats that surround Howland Island, several of which are listed or ranked by various authorities as being imperiled. Of note, the giant clam (*Tridacna maxima*) is abundant at Howland Island and is listed under the Convention on International Trade in Endangered Species of Wild Fauna and Flora (CITES). The humphead wrasse (*Cheilinus undulatus*) is also listed under CITES and designated as Endangered by the International Union for the Conservation of Nature (IUCN) and occurs in the nearshore waters of Howland. Nearshore waters are also home to two endangered species of sea turtles and sea mammals that have yet to be studied. Taken collectively with the terrestrial habitat, the coral reefs are an integral component of the overall health of the Howland Island ecosystem.

Corals

To date (January 2006), 97 species and 30 genera of corals and a few other large anthozoans have been reported from Howland reefs (Table B-1, Appendix B). Additional range extension records from collections and photographs may also exist. This compares to 92 species and 38 genera reported at neighboring Baker, only 32 nmi to the south. These totals are in the range of other atolls in the Phoenix Islands (Kanton *in* Maragos and Jokiel 1978); lower than, or comparable to similarly sized islands further to the west (Marshalls, Samoa); and higher than, or comparable to similarly sized islands to the east (Hawaii, Line Islands). There is no credible explanation for the higher genera totals at Baker compared to Howland, except that geographic isolation may be causing differential recruitment success. Supportive of this hypothesis is that 3 of the genera reported at Howland were missing at Baker, and 11 of the genera at Baker were missing from Howland. All sides of Baker have been surveyed compared to just the west and southeast side of Howland, and this may also be contributing to the higher generic diversity at Baker and discrepancies between the two reefs (Maragos per. comm.).

Corals are generally in healthy condition at Howland, with the eight most abundant genera there also the same as the eight most abundant found throughout the Line, Phoenix, and eastern Samoan Islands: *Acropora, Favia, Fungia, Leptoseris, Montipora, Pavona, Pocillopora,* and *Porites.* Coral disease prevalence and predation on corals are also low (G. Aeby and B. Vargas per. comm.). Although dead standing corals reported during the summer of 2000 were likely indicative of a coral bleaching event a few years earlier, no major bleaching event has been reported during the 2000-2006 surveys, and corals are presumably recovering rapidly during the period. Of future possible concern is the rapid expansion of the corallomorpharian *Rhodactis howesii* at Howland between the 2004 and 2006 staff visits near the historic boat anchorage. This species has increased to "invasive" proportions at Baker and Palmyra Atoll NWR where it appears to be stimulated by dissolved iron from corroding anchors or shipwrecks. Thus, it raises the possibility of corroding steel or iron being present at Howland Island which was observed in the form of chains and anchors at the western boat anchorage

Nearshore Fish

Approximately 324 species of reef fish are known from Howland reefs (Mundy et al. 2002; Table B-2, Appendix B). This compares with 247 species from nearby Baker. Moreover, ten families of fish reported at Howland have not been reported from Baker, and six minor families from Baker have not been reported from Howland. Of interest is the presence of several species of goby and scorpion fish families at Howland and the lack of these families at Baker. Possible explanations for these differences may be that sampling and survey intensities may be insufficient and different between the two islands, or that geographic isolation may result in differential recruitment rates between the two islands. As noted earlier, not all habitats at Howland have been surveyed to the same degree as those at Baker.

Reef fish populations appeared healthy and diverse with little indication of unauthorized harvest (Maragos, USFWS, per. comm.). However, during 2000 surveys Maragos noted many small sharks and no larger sharks at both Howland and Baker. In contrast, numerous small and some large sharks were at both locales by 2004 and 2006. Because "shark finning" (the catching of sharks only to remove their fins for sale) is a growing concern in the Pacific and other oceans, it is possible that a pre-2000 harvest of sharks at Howland resulted in the absence of larger adult sharks in 2000. Larger sharks and additional recruitment by 2004 and lack of subsequent shark fin harvest in the area may explain the more normal size distribution in sharks observed in 2004 and 2006 (Maragos et. al 2008b).

The fact that the disparities for the coral genera did not track in the same direction as for the fish families (more coral genera at Baker versus more fish families at Howland), reinforces the hypothesis of geographic isolation may lead to biodiversity heterogeneity based on chance and differential recruitment success. Geographic isolation would require both corals and reef fish to rely more on local recruitment vis-à-vis external recruitment. The latter would likely play a much larger role where reefs and islands are larger and closer together and result in similar biodiversity characteristics.

Marine Mammals

On most staff visits to Howland Island, a group of ~approximately 40 bottle-nosed dolphins (*Tursiops truncatus*) appear as the ship approaches the island. In 1993, individuals from this group were observed preying on rainbow runners (*Elagatis bipinnulatus*) that were sheltering under the vessel. Formal quantitative surveys of marine mammal distribution and abundance have not been undertaken at the refuge. Historically, sperm whales (*Physeter macrocephalus*) were caught near Howland in the nineteenth century (Townsend, 1935, cited in Sibley and Clapp, 1965).

Pelagic Wildlife

Oceanic pelagic fish including skipjack, yellowfin tuna, and blue marlin prefer warm surface layers, where the water is well mixed by surface winds and is relatively uniform in temperature and salinity. Other pelagic species, such as albacore, bigeye tuna, striped marlin, and swordfish, prefer cooler, more temperate waters, often meaning higher latitudes or greater depths. In fact, the largest proportion of the tuna catch in the Pacific Ocean originates from the warm pool, even though paradoxically this is a region of low primary productivity. Tuna movement to upwelling zones at the fringe of the warm pool may be key in resolving this apparent discrepancy between algal and tuna production. Preferred water temperature often varies with the size and maturity of pelagic fish, and adults usually have a wider temperature tolerance than subadults. Thus, during spawning, adults of many pelagic species usually move to warmer waters, the preferred habitat of their larval and juvenile stages.

Large-scale oceanographic events (such as El Niño) change the characteristics of water temperature and productivity across the Pacific, and these events have a significant effect on the habitat range and movements of pelagic species. Tuna are commonly most concentrated near islands and seamounts that create divergences and convergences, which concentrate forage species, and also near upwelling zones along ocean current boundaries and along gradients in temperature, oxygen, and salinity. Swordfish and numerous other pelagic species tend to concentrate along food-rich temperature fronts between cold upwelled water and warmer oceanic water masses (NMFS 2001). These frontal zones also function as migratory pathways across the Pacific for loggerhead turtles (Polovina et al. 2000). Loggerhead turtles are opportunistic omnivores that feed on floating prey such as the pelagic cnidarian, *Vellela vellela* ("by the wind sailor") and the pelagic gastropod *Janthina* spp., both of which are likely to be concentrated by the weak downwelling associated with frontal zones (Polovina et al. 2000).

The estimated hundreds of thousands of seabirds breeding at national wildlife refuges in the Central Pacific Ocean are primarily pelagic feeders that obtain the fish and squid they consume by associating with schools of large predatory fish such as tuna and billfish (Fefer et al. 1984, Au and Pitman 1986). These fish—yellowfin tuna (*Thunnus albacares*), skipjack tuna (*Katsuwonus pelamis*), mahimahi (*Coryphaena hippurus*), wahoo (*Acanthocybium solandri*), rainbow runner (*Elagatis bipinnulatus*), broadbilled swordfish (*Xiphias gladius*), and blue marlin (*Makaira indica*)—are apex predators of a food web existing primarily in the epipelagic zone. While both the predatory fish and the birds are capable of foraging throughout their pelagic ranges (which encompass the tropical Pacific Ocean), the birds are most successful at feeding their young when they can find schools of predatory fish within easy commuting range of the breeding colonies (Ashmole 1963, Feare 1976, Flint 1991). Recently fledged birds, inexperienced in this complex and demanding style of foraging, rely on abundant and local food resources to survive while they learn to locate and capture prey. Some evidence from tagging studies done by Itano and Holland (2000) suggests both yellowfin and bigeye tuna aggregate around island reef ledges, seamounts, and fish aggregating devices and are caught at a higher rate here than in open water areas. Yellowfin tuna in Hawai'i exhibit a summer island-related inshore-spawning run (Itano 2001).

Ashmole and Ashmole (1967) and Boehlert (1993) suggest that the circulation cells and wake eddies found downstream of oceanic islands may concentrate plankton and therefore enhance productivity near islands. Higher productivity, in turn, results in greater abundance of baitfish, thus allowing higher tuna populations locally. Johannes (1981) describes the daily migrations of skipjack tuna and yellowfin tuna to and from the waters near islands and banks. The presence of natural densities of these tunas within the foraging radius of seabird colonies enhances the ability of birds to provide adequate food for their offspring (Ashmole and Ashmole 1967; Au and Pitman 1986, Diamond 1978, Fefer et al. 1984.) Wake eddies also concentrate the larvae of many reef fishes and other reef organisms and serve to keep them close to reefs, enhancing survivorship of larvae and recruitment of juveniles and adults back to the reefs. For at least three of the seabird species breeding in the Central Pacific Ocean (brown noddies, white terns, and brown boobies), large proportions (33 to 56 percent) of their diets originate from the surrounding coral reef ecosystem, in other areas where their diet has been studied (Ashmole and Ashmole 1967; Harrison et al. 1983; King 1970; Diamond 1978).

Threatened and Endangered Species

Species listed under the Endangered Species Act documented at Howland include the threatened green turtle (*Chelonia mydas*) and the endangered hawksbill turtle (*Eretmochelys imbricata*). The Service shares responsibility with NMFS for these species. Both species have been observed and photographed foraging in the shallow water near the island.

Invasive Species

Human activities at Howland Island have resulted in various non-native species being introduced including the house cat (*Felis catus*), the Polynesian rat (*Rattus exulans*), various ant and cockroach species, and plants such as pandanus, ironwood, coconut palm, sea grape, ilima, *Portulaca oleracea,* and Pacific crabgrass. Feral cats were introduced in 1937 and finally eliminated in 1986. The rats were documented as early as 1854 and in many accounts were described as extremely abundant. Sometime after 1938, they were eliminated and have not been recorded since. Of the plants introduced by humans, only the Pacific crabgrass seems to have persisted. Although not achieving invasive proportions at Howland, the corallimorph *Rhodactis howesii* is already invasive at Baker and Palmyra and has the potential of becoming invasive at Howland and Kingman Reef especially near sites of metallic ship debris.

Wilderness Resources

Howland remains in a wilderness state in terms of its biota, seascape, and landscape except for the collection of abandoned fuel drums, excavations, and pits left behind from the guano mining era, and a small section of the reef blasted for a boat passage during the guano mining era. There was a makeshift airfield constructed in preparation for Amelia Earhart's last flight but today it is undistinguishable on the ground. A stone monument in her honor currently exists on the island. Abandoned anchors and chain may occur near the western boat passage. However, the collective contribution of these detractions is minor compared to the otherwise overwhelming wilderness character of the island and surrounding reefs. Additional wilderness information and evaluation are covered in greater detail in Appendix F.

Archaeology and Paleontology

Polynesians visited Howland Island prior to its discovery by European navigators (Hague 1862). Hague is the first to describe artifacts left by these earlier inhabitants. Among the artifacts described were excavations and mounds near the kou thicket in the center of the island, fragments of a canoe, footpaths, a blue bead, remains of a hut, and a human skeleton. The largest of the excavations was "several hundred feet long, and about one hundred feet wide, and ten or fifteen feet deep... [on each side of which the]... sand gravel [was] carefully banked up and kept in its place by walls laid up of coral stone."

Members of the Whippoorwill Expedition reexamined the ruins in 1924. Kenneth Emory (1939) remarked that the central excavation was of a sort commonly used in the Tuamotu Archipelago for growing taro, bananas, and sugar cane and that a canoe paddle was "exactly like a Tahitian paddle."

Howland had its first and only archaeological reconnaissance survey performed in 1987 (Shun 1987). This worked occurred on September 18-20, 1987, and consisted of only surface reconnaissance survey and limited subsurface testing performed as part of a U.S. Army Corps of Engineers Defense Environmental Restoration project to inventory and burn fuel in abandoned

World War II fuel drums on Baker and Howland Islands (Helene Takemoto per. comm.). The archaeological reconnaissance was done prior to the drum collection and burning to avoid possible damage to cultural resources (Shun 1987).

Environmental conditions on Howland are inhospitable to lengthy human occupation. A lack of a constant supply of fresh water is the primary limiting factor for habitation by humans. It is conceivable that early prehistoric people could have used Howland Island as a stopping, resting, or gathering place during their voyages across the Pacific Ocean, including capture of nesting sea turtles kept alive for extended food supply during long ocean voyages. However, it is doubtful that voyagers would have willingly settled on this island. Landings in any vessel would have been difficult, although access gained by small canoe is possible. Due to Howland Island's remoteness and lack of a sustainable freshwater supply, it is likely that Howland Island played a minimal role, if any, in the colonizing efforts of prehistoric people across the Pacific.

No records were found of paleontological surveys, although paleontological resources could exist in the form of fossilized coral or algae and other invertebrates. The chances of prehistoric indigenous terrestrial mammals inhabiting Howland Island are non-existent due to the geological forces that formed the island, its remoteness, and dry climate.

Recent Cultural History

The occupation and use of Howland Island after post-European contact, approximately AD 1800, can be divided into five distinctive time periods or eras based upon alternating periods of occupation, use, and abandonment. The eras are categorized as whaling, guano mining, colonizing, military, and post military.

Whaling Era: ca AD 1800-1850

Howland Island was initially called by various names and its first European discoverer remains unknown. At least three whaling vessels sighted or visited Howland Island during this period. The island was also known as "Worth" after Captain George B. Worth who viewed it from the whaling ship *Oeno* around 1822. Captain Daniel McKenzie of the New Bedford whaler, *Minerva Smith*, gave the island its present name. A quotation from McKenzie (*in* Maude 1961) explicitly states that he named the island for the owners of his ship. These owners were I. Howland, Jr. and Company (Starbuck 1878). However, it was Captain George E. Netcher of the whaling vessel *Isabella* who is generally credited for bestowing the island with its present name after the lookout who first saw it on September 9, 1842 (Bryan 1974). Thus, Howland Island appears to have been named Howland on two separate occasions.

Use of the island by whaling ship crews is speculative. Lacking an adequate harbor or sheltered bay, landings on the island are difficult to this day. However, whaling vessels may have stopped at Howland Island to acquire sea turtles, birds and eggs. Whalers also used nearby Baker Island and at times would leave letters and other correspondence.

Guano Mining Era: 1850-1891

On February 5, 1857, Alfred G. Benson and Charles H. Judd on board the Hawaiian schooner *Liholiho* officially claimed the island under the "Guano Act" of 1856 for the American Guano Company (Bryan 1974). Guano mining on Howland Island was delayed until after 1861 because of a mining rights dispute between the American Guano Company and United States Guano Companies, which was settled in favor of the American Guano Company. Mining on Howland Island peaked between 1870 and 1872 when, during a 4 month period in 1870, 7,600 tons of guano were off-loaded from the island in 109 working days, setting a record for guano mining in those days. An estimate of the total amount of guano removed varies between 85,000 to 100,000 tons (Bryan 1974). Evidence of this era of exploitation still remains as large basins from mining excavations and mounds of low-grade guano mark the island landscape.

Howland Island appears to have been abandoned from 1891 until 1935, although visits or very brief stopovers no doubt occurred during the interim. The Whippoorwill Expedition sponsored by Bishop Museum paid one such visit in September 1924. This scientific team spent 7 days on Howland Island, but a written record or log of the trip was not located during the development of this CCP.

Colonizing Era: 1935-1942

The establishment of trans-Pacific air routes; territorial ownership disputes over several islands in the Pacific between the United States and the United Kingdom in the early 1900s; and the threat of a second world war led to colonizing efforts by the United States on several Pacific Islands including Howland Island. Colonizing efforts began in March 1935. Several military personnel and graduates of Kamehameha Schools, Hawaii established a colony on Howland Island (Brown et al. 2002). After initial establishment, the colonists were comprised of Kamehameha graduates and were supplied with enough food, water and other necessities to sustain them "for a period of from six weeks to several months" (Bryan 1974). Water and bulk food were supplied from Hawaii. During this colonizing era, at least 26 trips were made to Howland Island by various United States Coast Guard (USCG) cutters. During the colonizing era, Howland Island was visited frequently and was often the scene of busy activity.

The colonists erected Itascatown as their place of permanent settlement. Other structures for water, food storage, radio equipment, and walls around the main settlement were constructed. Attempts to grow trees, flowers, and vegetables were tried but the climate was unfavorable for cultivated crops.

During this era, Amelia Earhart Putnam achieved national recognition as a pioneering aviator. Along with navigator Fred J. Noonan, they planned a circumnavigation of the world with a refueling stop on Howland Island. The U.S. Government, which had been planning to build an airfield on Howland Island, began construction of a runway in January 1937, so that it might be ready for the Earhart flight (Bryan 1974). By the time the airfield was completed, it consisted of three runways, 150 feet wide and of varying lengths. The North-South, East-West, and Northeast-Southwest runways were respectively 5,200 feet, 2,400 feet, and 3,000 feet long (Shun 1987).

On July 1, Amelia and Fred departed Lae, New Guinea hoping to complete the flight of approximately 2,250 miles to Howland Island in 18 to 20 hours. Somewhere between Lae, New Guinea and Howland Island, they vanished at sea. In the following 2 weeks, 10 ships and approximately 66 planes aided in the unsuccessful search for Amelia Earhart and Fred Noonan (Shun 1987).

Construction of a memorial to Amelia Earhart began on October 16, 1937, with the placement of the cornerstone for the Amelia Earhart light beacon (Bryan 1974).

Military Era: 1942-1944

The colony on Howland Island continued undisturbed except for routine USCG staff visits until December 8, 1941, when the island was bombed and machine-gunned by 14 Japanese planes. Some 60 bombs in all were dropped, but damage to the colonists' installations was negligible (Bryan 1974). Sadly, two colonists were killed. The island's surface was heavily scarred with some of the bombs leaving craters 20 feet across and 12 feet in depth on the surface of the island (Bryan 1974).

On December 10, a Japanese submarine surfaced offshore and fired approximately 50 shells into Itascatown, causing more damage than the initial bombing (Bryan 1974). The house and kitchen were destroyed and one shell hit the top of the Amelia Earhart light, rendering it useless. Two more aerial bombing attacks were made on the island on January 5 and January 24, 1942. The two survivors were removed from the island by the U.S. Navy destroyer *Helm* on January 31, 1942.

Howland Island was not visited again until September 13, 1943, when a military inspection team from nearby Baker Island reported that there were no bomb craters on the 2,400-foot strip and that all of the colonial installations had been rendered useless. The airstrip was subsequently readied for use for emergency landings (Shun 1987).

Post War Era: 1944 to Present

No attempt was made to re-colonize Howland Island after the war, although the Department of the Interior thought of doing so. In 1948, the U.S. decided that the claim to Howland Island could be effectively maintained by annual USCG staff visits. Thus, a USCG vessel apparently first visited the island after the war. Other USCG vessels that visited Howland Island included the *Kettle, Basswood, Buttonwood, Kukui,* the *Planetree, Blackhaw* and *Ironwood*. Most staff visits to Howland Island usually occurred in the first 4 months of the year with the ships' crews completing repairs to the day beacon and taking photographs to establish their presence on the Island. In 1963, the *Blackhaw* finally repaired the Earhart beacon destroyed 20 years earlier (Shun 1987).

In March 1963, and for the following 2 years, Smithsonian Institution employees made a number of staff visits to Howland Island as part of the SIPOBS (Sibley et al. 1965). During this period of investigation by the Smithsonian, a reconnaissance team of the AEC visited the island. This group arrived on Howland Island on October 14, 1963, conducted their survey for the following 3 days and departed. In addition, a survey by AEC was made of topographical, geological, and oceanographic features of the island.

In recent years, sporadic staff visits have occurred in the form of USCG and NOAA patrols and scientific expeditions. The island and its territorial seas were transferred to the Service in 1974 from the Department of the Interior Office of Insular Affairs. This area is now managed as a unit of the National Wildlife Refuge System. Refuge staff have participated in scientific expeditions, typically aboard NOAA vessels since 2000 and occurring once every 2 years since 2002.

Socio-economics

Historical Developments

Since whaling days, Howland Island has been used for a variety of commercial enterprises. During the whaling era, it appears that Howland Island served as a port-in-a-storm and possible gathering site for provisions by harvesting seabirds, sea turtles, and their eggs. Fishing for tuna and other species may also have occurred. The guano-mining era provided the world with a nutrient-rich fertilizer. Howland and other central Pacific islands were exploited for their deep guano deposits.

After the guano mining period, Howland Island was retained by the U.S. Government to aid in transportation and commerce during the mid-1930s. A colony was established on Howland Island to assert U.S. possession by placing 4 to 5 men on Howland Island from 1935 to 1942 (Bryan 1974, Brown et al. 2002). Howland Island was also used by the military during World War II as an emergency landing strip for operations on nearby Baker Island. After 1945, there was no further military use of the island, but USCG vessels performed annual patrols to protect U.S. economic interests in the central Pacific.

In modern times, a proposal to use of the island for military/atomic testing was developed in 1963 (AEC 1963), but the proposal did not materialize. In 1974, Howland Island and its territorial sea was transferred to the Service as a unit of the National Wildlife Refuge System to preserve and restore ecosystem values, focusing on nesting seabird populations

During the past decade, the government of Kiribati requested permission to allow their fishing fleets within Howland Island's 200-mile Exclusive Economic Zone (EEZ). The Department of the Interior relayed their concerns about this request to the appropriate offices of the Bureau of East Asian and Pacific Affairs in the Department of State. As a result, the Department of State informed the Government of Kiribati that the U.S. Government would decline that request. There are no current economic uses of Howland, and the island remains unpopulated.

Land Use

Howland Island has been uninhabited since the World War II era and would remain so except for occupation during periodic field camps. As such, the future "land use" for Howland Island would likely include establishing a temporary field camp site that would not conflict with important wildlife functions, habitat restoration, or wilderness values. Site planning would also identify corridors for small boat access, footpaths for regular island patrols, study sites, areas designated for solar power and potable water production generation, waste and trash disposal areas, work areas, and other needs.

Public Access

Howland is closed to public access. There has never been, nor are there plans to formally open the refuge to recreational activities by publishing public notice in the Federal Register. However, limited public access of Howland has been authorized in the past. Refuge access is managed through the issuance of a SUP when the activity is deemed compatible and appropriate with the purposes of refuge establishment.

Commercial Fishing

There has been essentially no recorded Hawaii-based longline fishing activity within the Howland and Baker Islands U.S. EEZs (0-200 nmi) from 1991-2007 (Hamm and Dowdell, 2008). There has also been no commercial purse seine fishing between 0-12 nmi around Howland and Baker Islands from 1998 to 2007 (NMFS SWFSC 2008). Over the years, foreign commercial fishing vessels may have targeted uninhabited Howland for unauthorized and illegal fishing because of the lack of on-site surveillance and enforcement capacity. The economic pressure to pursue this option would likely increase in the future as commercial fishing stocks in Asia and the Pacific become more heavily fished and depleted. Howland is habitat to many commercially valuable fishery species including sharks, lobsters, groupers, giant clams, tuna, wahoo, swordfish, deepwater snappers, bumphead parrotfish, humphead wrasses, various aquarium fish, pearl oysters, sea cucumbers, and other species. The no-take mandate and establishment of the refuge predated the applicability of the Magnuson-Stevens Fishery Conservation and Management Act of 1996 as amended (16 USC 1361 et seq.) to Howland. The deep slope area outside the refuge is likely too small to support commercial bottomfish harvest especially in light of the long commuting distances between Howland and the home ports of the fishing vessels.

APPENDICES

Appendix A. Glossary of Terms and Acronyms

ACHP. President's Advisory Council on Historic Preservation.

Alien species. Non-native species intentionally or accidentally introduced into habitats of the refuge.

Atoll. A tropical reef formation with a shallow water lagoon, surrounding perimeter reef, and reef islet(s).

Baker. Used alone in this report, it refers to the Baker Island National Wildlife Refuge.

CCP. Comprehensive Conservation Plan.

CCP/EA. A document that combines a Comprehensive Conservation Plan and an Environmental Assessment.

CFR. Code of Federal Regulations. A comprehensive directory of all Federal regulations.

CITES. Convention on the International Trade in Endangered Species of Wild Fauna and Flora.

Comprehensive Conservation Plan. A document that describes the desired future conditions of the refuge, and provides long-range guidance and management direction for the refuge manager to accomplish the purposes of the refuge, contribute to the mission of the System, and to meet other relevant mandates (Service Manual 602 FW 1.5).

CPWHP. Central Pacific World Heritage Project.

CRED. The Coral Reef Ecosystem Division of NOAA's Pacific Islands Fisheries Science Center.

DLNR. Hawaii Department of Land and Natural Resources.

DMA. Defense Mapping Agency.

EEZ. Exclusive Economic Zone.

EIS. Environmental Impact Statement. NEPA documentation that assesses the impacts of major Federal actions significantly affecting the quality of the human environment.

Environmental Assessment. A concise public document, prepared in compliance with the National Environmental Policy Act, that briefly discusses the purpose and need for an action, alternatives to such action, and provides sufficient evidence and analysis of impacts to determine whether to prepare an environmental impact statement or finding of no significant impact (40 CFR 1508.9).

ENSO. El Niño Southern Oscillation; a periodic ocean warming anomaly in the tropics.

EUC. Equatorial Undercurrent; a subsurface ocean current flowing east at the Equator.

Federal Register (FR). Official bulletin publicizing notices of Federal actions.

FMPS. Fishery Management Plans for commercial fisheries in Federal waters.

FONSI. Finding of No Significant Impact; a federal agency notice and preliminary decision that its proposed action would not require preparation of an EIS.

GIS. Geographic information system; a database integrating tabular and geographic data.

GPS. Global Positioning System; satellite-based for accurate geographic/site positioning.

Howland. Used alone in this report, it refers to the Howland Island National Wildlife Refuge.

Hydrophone. Underwater microphone or listening device.

Improvement Act. The National Wildlife Refuge System Improvement Act of 1997 amendment to the National Wildlife Refuge System Administration Act of 1966.

Insular Area. The current generic term used to refer to a United States possession, territory, Territory, freely associated state, or commonwealth under United States sovereignty.

Invasive Species. Either an alien or native species that spreads, or achieves dominance quickly, resulting in undesirable effects on native species and their habitats

ITCZ. Inter-tropical Convergence Zone; approximately along 5° N Latitude where the northeast and southeast tradewinds collide, rise, and create a zone of heavy rainfall and low winds; also known as the doldrums.

IUCN. International Union for the Conservation of Nature.

Jarvis. Used alone in this report, it refers to the Jarvis Island National Wildlife Refuge.

LEIS. Legislative Environmental Impact Statement. See EIS.

MBTA. Migratory Bird Treaty Act.

Mesoscale Eddy. A circular flow of water near an island or reef, roughly 10 to 100 nm in diameter caused by the wake of currents passing the reef or island.

µ L. Micro liter, or one-millionth of a liter.

NEC. North Equatorial Current, west-flowing surface current between 5-30°N Latitude.

NECC. North Equatorial Countercurrent; east-flowing surface current under the ITCZ.

NEPA. National Environmental Policy Act; establishes procedures requiring all Federal agencies to assess the environmental consequences of their actions.

NMI. Nautical mile; the equivalent of 1.15 statute (land) mile or 6,000 feet.

NMFS. The National Marine Fisheries Service of NOAA.

NOAA. National Oceanic and Atmospheric Administration.

NPS. National Park Service.

NWR. National Wildlife Refuge.

NWRS. National Wildlife Refuge System.

Oligotrophic. Waters having low levels of the mineral nutrients required by green plants. At Howland, this refers to the transparent zone of nutrient-poor shallow tropical waters, bounded by a thermocline serving as a barrier against exchange with deeper nutrient-rich waters.

Phenology. The study of periodic biological phenomena, such as breeding, flowering, and migrations, especially as related to climate.

Preferred Alternative. This is the alternative determined [by the decision maker] to best achieve the refuge purpose(s), vision, and goals; contributes to the Refuge System mission, addresses the issues; and is consistent with principles of sound fish and wildlife management.

Proposed Action. Preferred Alternative among several evaluated to comply with NEPA.

Quadrat. A rigid frame used by ecologists to facilitate unit area estimates of the size and density of surface-dwelling plants and animals; **Photo-quadrat.** A photograph of the area inside the quadrat to allow office data analysis after field staff visits.

PIFSC. NOAA's Pacific Islands Fisheries Science Center.

REA. Rapid ecological assessments.

Reef Island. Low tropical islet resting on a coral reef and consisting of reef rock and sand.

RONS. Refuge Operating Needs System; Service program for NWR operating funds.

ROV. Remotely operated vehicle; mobile un-manned device for collecting deep-sea data.

SAMMS. Service Asset Maintenance Management System; Service program to provide funds to maintain refuge property.

SEC. South Equatorial Current; westward-flowing ocean current driven by the southeast tradewinds between Latitudes 5° N and 30° S.

Secretary. The Secretary of the Interior.

Service. Used alone in this report, it refers to the U. S. Fish and Wildlife Service.

SIPOBS. Smithsonian Institution Pacific Ocean Biological Survey.

SUP. Special Use Permit; written Service approval and conditions for conducting an activity in a refuge.

System. Used alone in this report, it refers to the National Wildlife Refuge System.

Thermocline. In oceans, it is a depth zone of rapid density and temperature change serving as a barrier between mixing of shallow warmer surface and deeper subsurface waters.

Transect. A linear scientific field survey sampling design or area to facilitate repeatability, standard units of measurement, and future site relocation and resurvey.

UNESCO. United Nations Educational, Scientific and Cultural Organization.

USCG. United States Coast Guard.

U.S. Possession. Equivalent to *U.S. territory*. It is no longer current colloquial usage.

U.S. Territory. An incorporated United States insular area, of which only one currently exists, Palmyra Atoll, in which the United States Congress has applied the full body of the United States Constitution.

U.S. territory. A United States insular area in which the United States Congress has determined that only selected parts of the United States Constitution apply.

WESPAC. Western Pacific Regional Fisheries Management Council.

WSA. Wilderness Study Area.

World Heritage Property. A protected and inscribed natural and/or cultural site with "outstanding universal value" and meeting one or more of the eligibility criteria of the International Convention on World Heritage.

Appendix B. Species Lists

Table B-1: Corals and other cnidarians reported from Howland Island Refuge 1998-2006. After Maragos (2000-2003, 2004, 2006), and Maragos and Schmerfeld (1998)

Scientific Name	Common Name
MILLEPORIDAE	**Fire Corals**
Millepora platyphylla	fire coral
POCILLOPORIDAE	**Rose and Cauliflower Corals**
Pocillopora eydouxi	antler coral
Pocillopora meandrina	cauliflower or rose coral
Pocillopora verrucosa	knobby cauliflower coral
ACROPORIDAE	**Table, Plate, and Rice Corals**
Acropora cerealis	
Acropora cf. *clathrata*	
Acropora digitifera	
Acropora formosa	
Acropora gemmifera	
Acropora globiceps	
Acropora humilis	
Acropora hyacinthus	
Acropora latistella	
Acropora lukteni	
Acropora nasuta	
Acropora polystoma	
Acropora robusta	
Acropora secale	
Acropora subulata	
Acropora surculosa	
Acropora valida	
Acropora vaughani	Vaughan's staghorn coral
Acropora verweyi	Verwey's table coral
Montipora aequituberculata	
Montipora caliculata	
Montipora danae	
Montipora efflorescens	
Montipora foliosa	
Montipora foveolata	
Montipora hispida	
Montipora informis	
Montipora millepora	
Montipora cf. *patula*	

Scientific Name	Common Name
Montipora tuberculosa	
Montipora venosa	
Montipora cf. *verrilli*	
PORITIDAE	**Poritid Corals**
Porites annae	
Porites australiensis	
Porites lichen	lichen or yellow finger coral
Porites lobata	lobe or lobed porous coral
Porites lutea	mound coral
Porites rus	plate and pillar, or thin finger coral
Porites solida	solid or boulder coral
Porites sp.	
Porites vaughani	
Porites superfusa	
AGARICIIDAE	**Star Corals**
Gardineroseris planulata	honeycomb coral
Leptoseris mycetoseroides	
Pachyseris sp.	combed coral
Pavona explanulata	
Pavona minuta	disk coral
Pavona varians	corrugated coral
Pavona clavus	disk coral
FUNGIIDAE	**Mushroom Corals**
Cycloseris vaughani	Vaughan's mushroom coral
Fungia scutaria	mushroom coral
Fungia granulosa	mushroom coral
Fungia repanda	mushroom coral
Halomitra pileus	basket coral
Herpolitha limax	stone snake coral
Podabacia crustacea	
MUSSIDAE	**Spiny Brain Corals**
Symphyllia recta	colon coral
MERULINIDAE	**Knob corals**
Hydnophora rigida	
Hydnophora exesa	
Hydnophora microconos	
FAVIIDAE	**Brain Corals**
Cyphastrea serailia	small brain coral
Favia favus	
Favia matthaii	Matthai's brain coral
Favia pallida	
Favia rotumana	Rotuma's brain coral

Scientific Name	Common Name
Favia stelligera	
Favites pentagona	pentagonal brain coral
Favites complanata	
Favites flexuosa	
Favites russelli	Russell's brain coral
Favites sp.	
Goniastrea retiformis	
Goniastrea sp.	
Leptastrea pruinosa	
Leptastrea transversa	
Leptastrea bewickensis	Bewick's brain coral
Leptastrea purpurea	purple brain coral
Montastrea annuligera	
Montastrea curta	
DENDROPHYLLIIDAE	**Tube Corals**
Tubastraea coccinea	orange tube coral
ZOOANTHIDAE	**Zoanthid soft corals**
*Palythoa sp.	
DISCOSOMATIDAE	**Corallimorphs**
*Rhodactis howesii	red corallimorph
ALCYONARIA	**Octocorals**
*Lobophytum sp.	leather coral
*Sarcophyton sp.	leather coral
SIDERASTREIDAE	**Sandpaper corals**
Coscinaraea sp.	
Psammocora nierstraszi	
Psammocora profundacella	
Psammocora haimeana	
Psammocora stellata	
ANTIPATHARIA	**Black Corals**
Cirrhipathes sp.	wire coral

*indicates non-stony species

Table B-2: Shallow water records of fish collected from or observed at Howland Island from 1927-2002. Collected or compiled by Mundy et al. (2002).

Scientific Name	Common Name
GINGLYMOSTOMATIDAE	**Nurse Sharks**
Nebrius ferrugineus	nurse shark
CARCHARHINIDAE	**Requiem Sharks**
Carcharhinus amblyrhynchos	grey reef shark
Carcharhinus melanopterus	reef blacktip shark
Galeocerdo cuvieri	tiger shark
HEMIGALEIDAE	**Weasel Sharks**
Triaenodon obesus	reef whitetip shark
SPHYRNIDAE	**Hammerhead Sharks**
Sphyrna lewini	scalloped hammerhead shark
DASYATIDAE	**Sand Rays**
Taeniura meyeni	
MYLIOBATIDIDAE	**Eagle Rays**
Aetobatus narinari	spotted eagle ray
MOBULIDAE	**Manta Rays**
Manta sp.	manta
MURAENIDAE	**Moray Eels**
Anarchias allardicei	Allardice's moray
Anarchias cantonenesis	Canton Island moray
Echidna nebulosa	snowflake moray
Echidna polyzona	barred moray
Enchelycore pardalis	
Gymnomuraena zebra	zebra moray
Gymnothorax breedini	
Gymnothorax chilospilus	
Gymnothorax javanicus	giant moray
Gymnothorax flavimarginatus	yellow-margined moray
Gymnothorax marshallensis	Marshall Island moray
Gymnothorax meleagris	white-mouth moray
Gymnothorax picta	peppered moray
Gymnothorax rueppelliae	yellow-headed moray
Gymnothorax sp.	
Gymnothorax thyrsoideus	
Gymnothorax undulatus	undulated moray
Uropterygius sp.	
Uropterygius marmoratus	marbled snake moray
OPHICHTHIDAE	
Myrichthys maculosus	spotted snake eel
CONGRIDAE	**Conger Eel**
Conger sp.	

Scientific Name	Common Name
CHANIDAE	**Milkfish**
Chanos chanos	milkfish
SYNODONTIDAE	**Lizardfishes**
Synodus sp.	
HOLOCENTRIDAE	**Squirrelfishes**
Myripristis berndti	bigscale soldierfish
Sargocentron caudimaculatum	tailspot squirrelfish
Sargocentron diadema	crown squirrelfish
Sargocentrum microstoma	finelined squirrelfish
Sargocentrum punctatissimum	speckled squirrelfish
Sargocentrum tiere	blue-lined squirrelfish
SYNGNATHIDAE	**Pipefishes and Seahorses**
Choeroichthys sculptus	sculpted pipefish
AULOSTOMIDAE	**Trumpetfishes**
Aulostomus chinensis	trumpetfish
SCORPAENIDAE	**Scorpionfishes**
Pterois antennata	spotfin lionfish
Pterois radiate	clearfin lionfish
Petrois volitans	lionfish, turkeyfish
unidentified scorpionfish	
CARACANTHIDAE	**Orbicular Velvetfishes**
Caracanthus maculates	spotted coral croucher
SERRANIDAE	**Groupers & Sea Basses**
Aethaloperca rogaa	redmouth grouper
Cephalopholis argus	peacock grouper
Cephalopholis aurantia	
Cephalopholis miniata	coral grouper
Cephalopholis urodeta	flagtail grouper
Epinephelus fasciatus	black-tipped grouper
Epinephelus hexagonatus	hexagon grouper
Epinephelus howlandi	
Epinephelus macrospilos	black-spotted grouper
Epinephelus maculatus	highfin grouper
Epinephelus melanostigmus	blackspot honeycomb grouper
Epinephelus merra	honeycomb merra
Epinephelus retouti	
Epinephelus sp.	
Epinephelus spilotoceps	four-saddle grouper
Epinephelus tauvina	greasy grouper
Gracila albomarginata	white-margined grouper
Luzonichthys whitleyi	Whitley's slender basslet
Plectropomus laevis	Saddleback grouper

Scientific Name	Common Name
Pseudanthias bartlettorum	Bartlett's fairy basslet
Pseudanthias bartlettorum	
Pseudanthias cooperi	red-bar fairy basslet
Pseudanthias olivaceus	
Pseudantias sp.	
Variola louti	
ANTENNARIIDAE	**Frogfishes**
Antennarius tuberosus	
BELONIDAE	**Needlefishes**
Platybelone argulus platyura	keeled needlefish
Tylosurus crocodilus	crocodile needlefish
APOGONIDAE	**Cardinalfishes**
Apogon angustatus	broad-striped cardinalfish
Apogon apogonides	
Apogon coccineus	cryptic cardinalfish
Apogon fraenatus	bridled cardinalfish
Apogon luteus	
Cheilodipterus quinquelineatus	five-lined cardinalfish
MALACANTHIDAE	**Sand Tilefishes**
Malacanthus latovittatus	striped blanquillo
CORYPHAENIDAE	
Coryphaena hippurus	mahi mahi, common dolphinfish
ECHENEIDAE	**Remoras**
Echeneis sp.	
CARANGIDAE	**Jacks**
Carangoides ferdau	bar jack
Carangoides orthogrammus	yellow-spotted trevally
Caranx ignobilis	giant trevally
Caranx lugubris	black jack
Caranx melampygus	bluefin trevally
Caranx sexfasciatus	bigeye trevally
Elegatis bipinnulata	rainbow runner
Seriola dumerili	greater amberjack
Trachinotus baillonii	
LUTJANIDAE	**Snappers**
Aphareus furca	blue smalltooth jobfish
Aprion virescens	jobfish, uku
Lutjanus bohar	twinspot snapper, redspot snapper
Lutjanus fulvus	flametail snapper
Lutjanus gibbus	humpback snapper
Lutjanus kasmira	bluelined snapper
Lutjanus monostigma	onespot snapper

Scientific Name	Common Name
Macolor niger	black snapper
CAESIONIDAE	**Fusiliers**
Caesio teres	yellowback fusilier
Pterocaesio latovittata	yellowstreak fusilier
Pterocaesio marri	twinstripe fusilier
Pterocaesio tile	bluestreak fusilier
LETHRINIDAE	**Emperors**
Gnathodentex aureolineatus	yellowspot emperor
Monotaxis grandoculis	bigeye emperor
MULLIDAE	**Goatfishes**
Mulloides flavolineatus	yellowstripe goatfish
Mulloides mimicus (L. kasmira)	
Mulloides vanicolensis	yellowfin goatfish
Parupeneus bifasciatus	two-barred goatfish
Parupeneus cyclostomus	yellowsaddle goatfish
Parupeneus multifasciatus	multibarred goatfish
Parupeneus pleurostigma	sidespot goatfish
Parupeneus trifasciatus	
PRIACANTHIDAE	**Bigeyes**
Heteropriacanthus cruentatus	
PEMPHERIDAE	**Sweepers**
Pempheris oualensis	bronze sweeper
KYPHOSIDAE	**Chubs**
Kyphosus bigibbus	brown chub
Kyphosus cinerascens	highfin rudderfish
Kyphosus vaigiensis	lowfin rudderfish
Kyphosus sp.	
Sector ocyurus	
EPHIPPIDAE	**Batfishes**
Platax orbicularis	circular spadefish, batfish
Platax teira	longfin spadefish
CHAETODONTIDAE	**Butterflyfishes**
Chaetodon auriga	threadfin butterflyfish
Chaetodon citrinellus	speckled butterflyfish
Chaetodon kleinii	Klein's butterflyfish
Chaetodon lunula	racoon butterflyfish
Chaetodon meyeri	Meyer's butterflyfish
Chaedodon ornatissimus	ornate butterflyfish
Chaetodon quadrimaculatus	gourspot butterflyfish
Chaetodon reticulatus	reticulated butterflyfish
Chaetodon trifascialis	chevroned butterflyfish
Chaetodon unimaculatus	teardrop butterflyfish

Scientific Name	Common Name
Chaetodon vagabundus	vagabond butterflyfish
Forcipiger flavissimus	long-nosed butterflyfish
Forcipiger longirostris	big long-nosed butterflyfish
Hemitaurichthys thompsoni	Thompson's butterflyfish
Heniochus monoceros	masked bannerfish
Heniochus varius	humphead bannerfish
POMACANTHIDAE	**Angelfishes**
Apolemichthys griffisi	Griffis angelfish
Apolemichthys trimaculatus	three-spot angelfish
Apolemichthys xanthopunctatus	golden spotted angelfish
Centropyge bicolor	bicolor angelfish
Centropyge flavissima	lemonpeel angelfish
Centropyge flavissima vrolikii hyb.	Lemonpeel and Pearlscale angelfish hybrid
Centropyge loricula	flame angelfish
Centropyge vrolikii	pearlscale angelfish
Pomacanthus imperator	emporer angelfish
Pygoplites diacanthus	Regal angelfish
POMACENTRIDAE	**damselfishes**
Abudefduf notatus	yellow-tail sergeant
Abudefduf septemfasciatus	banded sergeant
Abudefduf sordidus	black-spot sergeant
Amphiprion chrysopterus	orange-fin anemonefish
Amphiprion perideraion	pink anemonefish
Chromis acares	midget chromis
Chromis agilis	bronze reef chromis
Chromis analis	yellow chromis
Chromis bicolor	
Chromis caudalis	blue axil chromis
Chromis margaritifer	bicolor chromis
Chromis vanderbilti	Vanderbilt's chromis
Chromis viridis (caerulea)	blue-green chromis
Chromis xanthura	black chromis
Chrysiptera glauca	gray demoiselle
Chry.brownriggii (leucopoma)	
Dascyllus auripinnis (ms)	
Lepidozygus tapeinosoma	Fusilier damsel
Plectroglyphidodon dickii	Dick's damsel
Plectroglyphidodon imparipennis	bright-eye damsel
Plectroglyphidodon johnstonianus	Johnston Island damsel
Plectroglyphidodon lacrymatus	jewel damsel
Plectroglyphidodon leucozonus	white-band damsel
Plectroglyphid. phoenixensis	Phoenix Islands damsel

Scientific Name	Common Name
Pomacentrus bankanensis	speckled damsel
Stegastes albifasciolatus	white-bar gregory
Stegastes aureus	
Stegastes fasciolatus	Pacific gregory
Stegastes nigricans	dusky farmerfish
KUHLIIDAE	**Flagtails**
Kuhlia petiti	
CIRRHITIDAE	**Hawkfishes**
Cirrhiticythys aprenius	
Cirrhitichthys falco	falco hawkfish
Cirrhitichthys oxycephalus	pixy hawkfish
Cirrhitops hubbardsi	
Cirrhitus pinnulatus	stocky hawkfish
Neocirrhites armatus	flame hawkfish
Paracirrhites arcatus	arc-eye hawkfish
Paracirrhites forsteri	freckled hawkfish
Paracirrhites hemistictus	whitespot hawkfish
SPHYRAENIDAE	**Barracudas**
Sphyraena barracuda	great barracuda
LABRIDAE	**Wrasses**
Anampses caeruleopunctatus	blue-spotted wrasse
Anampses meleagrides	yellowtail wrasse
Anampses twistii	yellowbreasted wrasse
Bodianus axillaries	axilspot hogfish
Bodianus dianna	Diana's hogfish
Bodianus prognathus	
Cheilinus oxycephalus	snooty wrasse
Cheilinus trilobatus	tripletail wrasse
Cheilinus undulatus	humphead wrasse, napoleonfish
Cirrhilabrus exquisitus	exquisite wrasse
Coris aygula	clown coris
Coris centralis	
Coris gaimard	yellowtail coris
Gomphosus varius	bird wrasse
Halichoeres hortulanus	checkerboard wrasse
Halichoeres margaritaceus	weedy surge wrasse
Halichoeres melasmopomus	black-ear wrasse
Halichoeres ornatissinus	ornate wrasse fish
Halichoeres scapularis	zigzag wrasse
Halichoeres trimaculatus	three-spot wrasse
Hemigymnus fasciatus	barred thicklip wrasse
Labroides bicolor	bicolor cleaner wrasse

Scientific Name	Common Name
Labroides dimidiatus	bluestreak cleaner wrasse
Labroides pectoralis	black-spot cleaner wrasse
Labroides rubrolabiatus	
Labropsis xanthonota	wedge-tailed wrasse
Macropharyngodon meleagris	leopard wrasse
Novaculichtyhs taeniourus	dragon wrasse, rockmover wrasse
Oxycheilinus unifasciatus	
Oxycheilinus evanidus	
Pseudocheilinus hexataenia	sixline wrasse
Pseudocheilinus octotaenia	eightline wrasse
Pseudocoris heteroptera	
Pseudodax mollucanus	
Stethojulis bandanensis	red-shoulder wrasse
Thalassoma amblycephalum	two-tone wrasse
Thalassoma lutescens	sunset wrasse
Thalassoma purpureum	surge wrasse
Thalassoma quinquevittatum	five-stripe surge wrasse
Thalassoma trilobatum	Christmas wrasse
SCARIDAE	**Parrotfishes**
Bolbometopon muricatum	humphead parrotfish
Calatomus carolinus	bucktooth parrotfish, stareye parrotfish
Chlorurus microrhinus	
Chlorurus sordidus	
Scarus altipinnis	filament-finned parrotfish
Scarus frenatus	vermiculate parrotfish
Scarus niger	black parrotfish
Scarus oviceps	dark-capped parrotfish
Scarus rubroviolaceus	red and violet parrotfish
Scarus tricolor	
Scarus sp.	
TRIPTERYGIIDAE	**Triplefins**
Enneapterygius sp	
Enneapterygius nigricada	
Helcogramma chica	
BLENNIIDAE	**Blennies**
Blenniela caudolineata	
Blenniella gibbifrons	
Blenniella paula	
Cirripectes polyzona	barred blenny
Cirripectes quagga	squiggly blenny
Cirripectes sp.	
Cirripectes variolosus	red-speckled blenny

Scientific Name	Common Name
Ecsenius midas	
Entomacrodus sp.	
Entomacrodus striatus	
Exallias brevis	
Istiblennius sp.	
Istiblennius edentulous	rippled rockskipper
Istiblennius lineatus	lined rockskipper
Plagiotremus rhynorhynchus	bluestriped blenny
Plagiotremus tapeinosoma	piano blenny, Scale-eating blenny
Rhabdoblennius rhabdotrachelus	
GOBIESOCIDAE	**Clingfishes and Singleslits**
Lepidichthys minor	
GOBIIDAE	**Gobies**
unid. goby cf. *Eviota viridis*	
Bathygobius cocosensis	Cocos frill goby
Bathygobius fuscus	fusky frill goby
Eviota sp.	
Eviota epiphanies	small sleeper
Eviota saipanensis	Saipan pygmy goby
Eviota viridis	
Gnatholepis sp.	
Priolepis semidoliatus	
Priolepis squamogena	
Valenciennea strigata	
CALLIONYMIDAE	**Dragonets**
Synchiropus sp.	mandarin fish
PTERELEOTRIDAE	**Dartfishes**
Ptereleotris evides	
ACANTHURIDAE	**Surgeonfishes & Unicornfishes**
Acanthurus Achilles	Achilles tang
Acanthurus blochii (mata)	ringtail surgeonfish
Acanthurus guttatus	spotted surgeonfish
Acanthurus lineatus	
Acanthurus maculiceps	White-freckled surgeonfish
Acanthurus mata	elongate surgeonfish
A. nigricans (glaucopareius)	whitecheek surgeonfish
Acanthurus nigricauda	epaulette surgeonfish
Acanthurus nigrofuscus	brown surgeonfish
Acanthurus nigroris	blue-lined surgeonfish
Acanthurus nubilis	
Acanthurus olivaceus	orangeband surgeonfish
Acanthurus pyroferus	chocolate surgeonfish

Scientific Name	Common Name
Acanthurus rackliffei	
Acanthurus triostegus	
Acanthurus thompsoni	Thompson's surgeonfish
Acanthurus xanthopterus	yellow-finned surgeonfish
Acan. achilles x nigricans	
Acanthurus sp.	
Ctenochaetus cyanocheilus	
Ctenochaetus flavicaudis	
Ctenochaetus hawaiiensis	chevron tang, black surgeonfish
Ctenochaetus marginatus	blue-spotted bristletooth
Ctenochaetus striatus	striped bristletooth
Naso brevirostris	spotted unicornfish
Naso hexacanthus	blacktongue unicornfish , sleek unicornfish
Naso lituratus	liturate surgeonfish
Naso vlamingii	bignose unicornfish
Naso sp.	
Paracanthurus hepatus	palette surgeonfish, hepatus tang
Zebrasoma rostratum	
Zebrasoma scopas	brown tang
Zebrasoma veliferum	Sailfin tang
ZANCLIDAE	**Moorish Idol**
Zanclus cornutus	moorish idol
ISTIOPHORIDAE	**Billfishes**
SCOMBRIDAE	**Tunas**
Euthynnus affinis	kawakawa, bonito
Gymnosarda nuda	dogtooth tuna
Thunnus albacares	yellowfin tuna
BOTHIDAE	**Left-hand Flounders**
Bothus mancus	peacock flounder
BALISTIDAE	**Triggerfishes**
Balistapus undulatus	orangestriped triggerfish
Ballistoides conspicillum	Clown triggerfish
Balistoides viridescens	mustache triggerfish, titan triggerfish
Melichtys niger	Black triggerfish
Melichtys vidua	pinktail triggerfish
Odonus niger	redtooth triggerfish
Pseudobalistes flavimarginatus	yellowmargin triggerfish
Rhinecanthus rectangulus	wedge picassofish, humuhumu
Sufflamen bursa	scythe triggerfish, boomerang triggerfish
Sufflamen chrysopterus	halfmoon triggerfish
Sufflamen frenatus	Bridle triggerfish
Xanthichthys auromarginatus	bluechin triggerfish, guilded triggerfish

Scientific Name	Common Name
Xanthichthys caeruleolineatus	bluelined triggerfish
MONACANTHIDAE	**Filefishes**
Aluterus scriptus	scribbled filefish
Amanses scopas	broom filefish
Cantherhines dumerilii	barred filefish
Cantherhines pardalis	wire-net filefish
OSTRACIIDAE	**Trunkfishes**
Ostracion meleagris	spotted trunkfish
TETRAODONTIDAE	**Puffers**
Arothron hispidus	whitespotted puffer
Arothron meleagris	guineafowl puffer
Canthigaster amboinensis	Ambon sharpnose puffer
Canthigaster janthinoptera	
Canthigaster solandri	spotted sharpnose puffer
DIODONTIDAE	**Porcupinefishes**
Diodon hystrix	porcupinefish
Diodon liturosis	shortspine porcupinefish

Table B-3: Plant species of Howland Island NWR. Compiled from unpublished USFWS trip reports.

Scientific Name	Common Name, (Hawaiian Name)	Source*	Observed by**	Observed in 2004
Cocos nucifera	coconut, (niu)	I		no
Casuarina sp.	Ironwood	I		no
Pandanus sp.	pandanus, (hala)	I		no
Digitaria pacifica	Pacific crabgrass	A	d,e	yes
Lepturus repens	Pacific Island thintail	N	a,b,c,d,e	yes
Boerhavia sp.	alena	N	a,b,c,d,e	yes
Portulaca lutea	portulaca, 'ihi	N	a,b,d,e	yes
Portulaca oleracea	portulaca, 'ihi	A	a,b,d,e	yes
Sophora tomentosa	yellow neclacepod	W	E	no
Tribulus cistoides	puncturevine, nohu	N	a,b,c,d,e	yes
Cordia subcordata	cordia, kou	N	a,c,d,e	yes
Coccoloba uvifera	sea grape	I	c,d,e	no
Sida fallax	'ilima	A	E	no
Scaevola taccada	naupaka	W	F	yes
Suriana maritime	bay cedar	W	F	yes
Tournefortia argentea	tree heliotrope	W	g	yes

*Source: N = native, I = introduced, A = accidentally introduced, W = wave carried
** Collectors and Observers:

a - E. Christophersen 1924   e - C.R. Long 1964
b - E.H. Bryan 1938   f - Rauzon and Woodside 1998
c - F. Sibley 1963   g - Depkin and Newton 1995
d - P. Marshall 1963

Table B-4: Birds of Howland Island NWR. Numbers are counts of adult birds only and compiled from unpublished USFWS trip reports. Note: No bird species found on Howland are listed according to the Endangered Species Act.

Scientific Name	Common Name	Highest count since 1973	Birds of Conservation Concern Status[b]	National Shorebird Prioritization Category[a]	Regional Seabird Conservation Category[c]
Nesofregetta fuliginosa	Polynesian storm-petrel	-	BCC 68		Highly Imperiled
Pterodroma alba	Phoenix petrel	-	BCC 68		Highly Imperiled
Puffinus pacificus	wedge-tailed shearwater	1			Low
Phaethon lepturus	white-tailed tropicbird	1			Low
Phaethon rubricauda	red-tailed tropicbird*	496			Moderate
Sula dactylatra	masked booby*	3,763			Moderate
Sula leucogaster	brown booby*	275			Moderate
Sula sula	red-footed booby*	825			Currently not at Risk
Fregata minor	great frigatebird*	550			Moderate
Fregata ariel	lesser frigatebird*	3,850	BCC 68		High Concern
Onychoprion lunata	gray-backed tern*	2,000			Moderate
Onychoprion fuscatuc	sooty tern*	150,000			Moderate
Anous stolidus	brown noddy*	1,000			Currently not at Risk
Procelsterna cerulea	blue-grey noddy*	11	BCC 68		High Concern
Gygis alba	white tern*	50			Moderate
Pluvianlis dominica	Pacific golden-plover	126	BCC 68	High Concern	
Tringa incana	wandering tattler	27		Moderate Concern	
Numenius tahitiensis	bristle-thighed curlew	62	BCC 68	High Concern	
Arenaria interpres	ruddy turnstone	141		High Concern	

Scientific Name	Common Name	Highest count since 1973	Birds of Conservation Concern Status[b]	National Shorebird Prioritization Category[a]	Regional Seabird Conservation Category[c]
Limosa lapponica	bar-tailed godwit	1		High Concern	
Calidris acuminata	sharp-tailed sandpiper	1			
Calidris melanotos	pectoral sandpiper	1			
Calidris alba	sanderling	1			
Bubuculus ibis	cattle egret	-			
Anas acuta	northern pintail	14			

*indicates documented breeding species on Howland

[a]Species prioritization categories according to United States Shorebird Conservation Plan (Brown et al. 2000)

[b]Birds of Conservation Concern status according to Birds of Conservation Concern 2002 (U.S. Fish and Wildlife Service 2002).

[c]Conservation classification according to Seabird Conservation Plan, Pacific Region (Englis and Naughton 2004)

Appendix C. References

Ashmole, N.P. 1963. The biology of the Wide-awake or Sooty Tern (*Sterna fuscata*) on Ascension Island. *Ibis* 103b: 297-364.

Ashmole, N.P., and M.J Ashmole. 1967. Comparative Feeding Ecology of Sea Birds of a Tropical Oceanic Island. Peabody Museum of Natural History, Yale University Bulletin 24.

Atomic Energy Commission. 1963. Reconnaissance Survey Report: Howland, Baker & Canton Islands. Las Vegas, NV.

Au, D.K., and R.L. Pitman. 1986. Seabird Interactions with Dolphins and Tuna in the Eastern Tropical Pacific. *The Condor* 88 (3): 304-317.

Baker, J.D., C.L. Littnan, D.W. Johnston. 2006. Potential effects of sea level rise on the terrestrial habitats of endangered and endemic megafauna in the Northwestern Hawaiian Islands. Endangered Species Research 2: 21-30.

Boehlert, G. 1993. Fisheries and marine resources of Hawaii and the U.S.-associated Pacific Islands: an introduction. *Marine Fisheries Review* 55: 3-7.

Brown, D, N.M.K.Y. Kahanu, S.K. Kikiloi, T.K. Tengan and J. Zisk. 2002. Hui Panalāʻau. Bishop Museum, Honolulu, published pamphlet, 16 pp.

Brown, S., C. Hickey, and B. Harrington eds. 2000. The U.S. Shorebird Conservation Plan. Manomet Center for Conservation Sciences, Manomet, MA.

Browne, A.C. 1940. Proc. Hawaiian Ent. Soc. 10(3):369.

Bryan, E.H., Jr. 1974. Panala'au Memoirs. Pacific Scientific Information Center. Bernice P. Bishop Museum, Honolulu, HI.

Buddemeier, R.W., J.A. Kleypas, and R.B. Aronson. 2004. Coral reefs and global climate change: Potential contributions of climate change to stresses on coral reef ecosystems. Pew Centre for Global Climate Change: Arlington, VA.

Carter T. R., La Rovere, E.L., Jones, R.N., Leemans, R., Mearns, L.O., Nakicenovic, N., Pittock, A.B., Semenov, S.M., and Skea, J. 2001. Developing and Applying Scenarios. In IPCC 2001: Climate Change 2001: Impacts, Adaptation, and Vulnerability. CUP, Cambridge, UK.

Christophersen, E. 1927. Vegetation of Pacific Equatorial Islands. Bernice P. Bishop Museum Bulletin 44: No. 2. 79 p.

Citta, John, and Michelle H. Reynolds. 2006. Draft Seabird Monitoring Assessment for Hawaii and the Pacific Islands. Migratory Birds and Habitat Programs USFWS. USGS-BRD 183 pp.

Cobb K.M., C.D. Charles, H. Cheng, and R.L. Edwards. 2003. El Niño/Southern Oscillation and tropical Pacific climate during the last millennium. Nature 424: 271-276.

D'Arrigo, R., E. Cook, R. Wilson, A. Tudhope, C. Deser, G. Wiles, R. Villalba, J. Cole, and B. Linsley. 2005. Tropical–North Pacific Climate Linkages over the Past Four Centuries. Journal of Climate 18:5253-5265.

Darwin, C. 1842. The structure and distribution of coral reefs. Smith Elder, London. 214 pp., 2 pls.

Depkin, C., and C. Newton. 1995. Howland Island Trip Report 22-25 March 1995. Administrative Report. U.S. Fish and Wildlife Service, Honolulu, HI.96850.

Diamond, A.W. 1978. Feeding strategies and population size in tropical seabirds. American Naturalist 112:215-223.

Emory, K.P. 1939. Archaeology of the Phoenix Islands. Hawaii Academy of Science Proceedings. Special Publication 34, Bishop Museum, Honolulu, HI.

Engilis, Jr., A. and M. Naughton. 2004. U.S. Pacific Islands Regional Shorebird Conservation Plan. U.S. Shorebird Conservation Plan. U.S. Department of the Interior, Fish and Wildlife Service, Portland, OR.

Ehleringer, J.R., T.E. Cerling, and M.D. Dearing. 2002. Atmospheric CO_2 as a global change driver influencing plant-animal interactions. Integrated and Comparative Biology 42:424–430.

Feare, C.J. 1976. The breeding of the Sooty Tern *Sterna fuscata* in the Seychelles and the effects of experimental removal of its eggs. *Journal of Zoology, London* 179: 317–360.

Feeley, R.A., C.L. Sabine, K. Lee, W. Berelson, J. Kleypas, V.J. Fabry, and F.J. Millero. 2004. Impact of anthropogenic Co2 on the CaCO3 system in the oceans. Science 305:362-366.

Fefer, S.I., C.S. Harrison, M.B. Naughton, and R.J. Shallenberger. 1984. Synopsis of results of recent seabird research conducted in the Northwestern Hawaiian Islands. Proc. Res. Inv. NWHI UNIHI-SEAGRANT-MR-84-01

Fish, M.R., I.M. Côté, J.A. Gill, A.P. Jones, S. Renshoff, A.R. Watkinson. 2005. Predicting the impact of sea level rise on Caribbean sea turtle nesting habitat. Conservation Biology 19: 482–491.

Flint, E. 1991. Time and energy limits to the foraging radius of sooty terns *Sterna fuscata*. *Ibis*. 133: 43-46.

Flint, E., and D. Woodside. 1993. Howland and Baker Islands Trip Report, 19 January to 15 February, 1993. Administrative Report, U.S. Fish and Wildlife Service, Honolulu, HI.

Flint, E., and C. Eggleston. 2004. Draft Equatorial Refuges Trip Report. January 8-31, 2004. Administrative Report. U.S. Fish and Wildlife Service, Honolulu, HI.

Floros, C.D., M.J. Samways, and B. Armstrong. 2004. Taxonomic patterns of bleaching within a South African coral assemblage. Biodiversity and Conservation. 13:1175-1194, Fowler1927.

Grimsditch, G.D., and R.V. Salm. 2005. Coral reef resilience and resistance to bleaching. The World Conservation Union. Gland, CH.

Hague, J.D. 1862. On phosphatic guano islands of the Pacific Ocean. Amer. Jour. Sci., 84: 224-243, 1862.

Hamm, D., and F. Dowdell. 2008. Summary of the Hawaii-based Longline Logbook Data for Catches in the EEZs of Howland, Baker, and Jarvis Islands. National Marine Fisheries Service Pacific Islands Fisheries Science Center. PIFSC Internal Report IR-08-008. 4 pp.

Hansen, James, M. Sato, P. Kharecha, D. Beerling, V. Masson-Delmotte, M. Pagani, M. Raymo, D.L. Royer, and J.C. Zachos. 2008. Submitted. Target Atmospheric CO_2: Where Should Humanity Aim? Science.

Harrison, C.S., T.S. Hida, M.P. Seki. 1983. Hawaiian Seabird Feeding Ecology. Wildlife Monographs 85:1-71.

Hutchinson, G.E. 1950. The Biochemistry of Vertebrate Excretion. Bull. Amer. Museum Nat. Hist. 96. 554 p.

IPCC (Intergovernmental Panel on Climate Change), Ed. 2001. Climate Change 2001: The Scientific Basis, Contribution of Working Group I to the Third Assessment Report of the Intergovernmental Panel on Climate Change. Cambridge Univ. Press, Cambridge, UK. 881 pp.

IPCC. 2001. Working group II to the third assessment report, climate change 2001: Impacts, adaptation, and vulnerability. Cambridge Univ. Press, Cambridge, UK.

IPCC. 2007a. *Climate Change 2007* The physical science basis. Contribution of working group I to the fourth assessment report of the intergovernmental panel on climate change. Fourth assessment report of the intergovernmental panel on climate change. [Solomon, S., D. Qin, M. Manning, Z. Chen, M. Marquis, K.B. Averyt, M. Tignor, and H.L. Miller eds.]. Cambridge University Press, Cambridge, UK, and New York, NY, USA. 996 pp.

IPCC. 2007b. Working group II to the third assessment report, Climate Change 2007: Impacts, adaptation, and vulnerability. Cambridge University Press, Cambridge, UK.

Itano, D.G., and K.N. Holland. 2000. Movement and vulnerability of bigeye (*Thunnus obesus*) and yellowfin tuna (*Thunnus albacares*) in relation to FADs and natural aggregation points. *Aquat. Living Resour.* 13: 213–223.

Itano, D.G. 2001. The Reproductive biology of yellowfin tuna (*Thunnus albacares*) in Hawaiian waters and the Western Tropical Pacific Ocean: Project summary. SOEST Publication 00-01, JIMAR Contribution 00-328, University of Hawai'i, Honolulu, HI. 69 pp.

Johannes, R.E. 1981. Words of the Lagoon: Fishing and marine lore in the Palau District of Micronesia. University of California Press, Berkeley, CA.

Kayanne, H., T. Ishii, E. Matsumoto, and N. Yonekura. 1993. Late Holocene sea-level change on Rota and Guam, Mariana Islands, and its constraint on geophysical predictions. Quaternary Research 40:189-200.

King, W.B. 1970. The trade wind zone oceanography pilot study. Part VII: observations of seabirds March 1964 to June 1965. U.S. Fish and Wildl. Ser. Spec. Sci. Rep. - Fish. 586. 136pp.

Kirkpatrick R.D., and M.J. Rauzon. 1986. Foods of Feral Cats *Felis catus* on Jarvis and Howland Islands, Central Pacific Ocean. Biotropica 18 (1): 72-75.

Levitus, S., J. Antonov, and T. Boyer. 2005. Warming of the world ocean, 1955-2003. Geophysical Research Letters 32, L02604, doi:10.1029/2004GL021592.

Maude, H.E. 1961. Post-Spanish discoveries in the central Pacific. Jour. Pol. Soc. 70(1):67-111.

Maragos, J.E. 2008. Coral response to anthropogenic and natural stresses at 7 Pacific Remote Island National Wildlife Refuges from 1999-2007: Vignettes from selected permanent monitoring transects. State of the coral reefs of the United States and the Freely Associated States: 2008. J. Waddell, ed. NOAA Technical Memorandum NOS NCCOS, Silver Spring, MD, in press.

Maragos, J., J. Miller, J. Gove, E. DeMartini, A. Friedlander, S. Godwin, C. Musburger, M. Timmers, R. Tsuda, P. Vroom, E. Flint, E. Lundblad, J. Weiss, P. Avotte, E. Sala, S. Sandin, S. McTee, T. Wass, D. Siciliano, R. Brainard, D. Obura, S. Ferguson, and B. Mundy. 2008a. U.S. coral reefs in the Line and Phoenix Islands, Central Pacific Ocean: History, Geology, Oceanography, and Biology. In: Riegl, B. and Dodge R.E. (eds) *Coral Reefs of the USA. Coral Reefs of the World, Volume 1*, Springer-Verlag, pp 591-638

Maragos, J., A. Friedlander, S. Godwin, C. Musburger, E. Flint, O. Pantos, E. Sala, and S. Sandin. 2008b. U.S. coral reefs in the Line and Phoenix Islands, Central Pacific Ocean: Status, Threats and Significance. In: Riegl, B. and Dodge R.E. (eds) *Coral Reefs of the USA. Coral Reefs of the World, Volume 1*, Springer–Verlag, pp 639-650

Maragos, J.E., and P.L. Jokiel. 1978. Reef Corals of Canton Atoll: I. Zoogeography. In: Naval Undersea Center Technical Publication 395:55-70, and *Atoll Research Bulletin* 221:55-70 (Sept 1978)

Michener, W.K., E.R. Blood, K.L. Bildstein, M.M. Brinson, and L.R. Gardner. 1997. Climate change, hurricanes and tropical storms and rising sea level in coastal wetlands. Ecological Applications. 7:770-801.

Miller, J., J. Maragos, R. Brainard, J. Asher, B. Vargas-Angel, J. Kenyon, R. Schroeder, B. Richards, M. Nadon, P. Vroom, A. Hall, E. Keenan, M. Timmers, J. Gove, E. Smith, J. Weiss, E. Lundblad, S. Ferguson, F. Lichowski and J. Rooney. The State of Coral Reef Ecosystems of the Pacific Remote Island Areas. In: State of the coral reefs of the United States and the Freely Associated States: 2008. J. Waddell, ed. NOAA Technical Memorandum NOS NCCOS, Silver Spring, MD, in press.

Mueller-Dombois, D., and F.R. Fosberg. 1998. Vegetation of the Tropical Island Pacific. Springer-Verlag, New York (Book in collection of H. Freifeld, 3-122 Federal Building).

Morrison, R.J. 1990. Pacific Atoll Soils: Chemistry, Mineralogy and Classification. Atoll Research Bulletin. No. 339: 25p.

Mundy, B., R. Wass, E. DeMartini, B. Greene, B. Zgliczynski, and R. Schroeder. 2002. Inshore fishes of Howland Island, Baker Island, Jarvis Island, Palmyra Atoll, and Kingman Reef. Unpublished ms. Pacific Islands Fisheries Science Center, Honolulu, HI. 80 pp.

Munro, G.C. 1924. (unpublished) Report of the ornithologist on the USS Whippoorwill expedition trip "B" to Howland and Baker Islands. Sept. 15 to Oct. 7, 1924. (Extracted Aug. 4, 1965, by Roger Clapp).

National Marine Fisheries Service and U.S. Fish and Wildlife Service. 1998. Recovery Plan for U.S. Pacific Populations of the Green Turtle (*Chelonia mydas*). National Marine Fisheries Service, Silver Springs, MD.

National Marine Fisheries Service and U.S. Fish and Wildlife Service. 1998. Recovery Plan for U.S. Pacific Populations of the Hawksbill Turtle (*Eretmochelys imbricate*). National Marine Fisheries Service, Silver Springs, MD.

National Marine Fisheries Service - Southwest Fisheries Science Center. 2008. Number of Purse Seine Vessels, Number of Sets and Total Catch (metric tons) for the Pacific Remote Insular Areas Divided into 4 Bands Around Each Island. South Pacific Tuna Treaty Program. 6 pp.

Nicholls, R.J., P.P. Wong, V.R. Burkett, J.O. Codignotto, J.E. Hay, R.F. McLean, S. Ragoonaden, and C.D. Woodroffe. 2007. Coastal systems and low-lying areas. Climate change 2007: impacts, adaptation and vulnerability. Pages 315-356 *in* Parry, M.L., O.F. Canziani, J.P. Palutikof, P.J. van der Linden and C.E. Hanson (editors). Contribution of working group II to the fourth assessment report of the intergovernmental panel on climate change. Cambridge University Press, Cambridge, UK.

NOAA. 1991. Climates of the World. Historical Climatology Series 6-4. National Oceanic and Atmospheric Administration, National Climatic Data Center, Asheville, N.C. p. 26.

OPIC (Overseas Private Investment Corporation). 2000. Climate change: assessing our actions. Agency of the United States Government. Washington, DC.

Overpeck, J.T., B.L. Otto-Bliesner, G.H. Miller, D.R. Muhs, R.B. Alley, and J.T. Kiehl. 2006. Paleoclimatic Evidence for Future Ice-Sheet Instability and Rapid Sea-Level Rise. Science 311:1747-1750.

Parmesan, C. 2006. Ecological and Evolutionary Responses to Recent Climate Change. Annu. Rev. Ecol. Evol. Syst. 37:637-69.

Paulay, G. and Y. Benayahu. 1999. Patterns and consequences of coral bleaching in Micronesia (Majuro and Guam) in 1992-1994. Micronesica 32: 109-124.

Porter, V., T. Leberer, M. Gawel, J. Gutierrez, D. Burdick, V. Torres, and E. Lujan. 2005. The state of coral reef ecosystems of Guam. Pages 442-487 *in* The state of coral reef ecosystems of the United States and Pacific freely associated states: 2005. National Oceanic and Atmospheric Administration (NOAA).

Prasad, U.K., and H.I. Manner. 1994. Climate change and sea level rise issues in Guam. Report on a preliminary mission. Apia, Western Samoa: South Pacific Regional Environmental Programme. SPREP Reports and Studies Series No. 82.

Rauzon, M.J., and D.H. Woodside. 1998. Howland Island Trip Report26 4-9 March 1998. Administrative Report. U.S. Fish and Wildlife Service, Honolulu, HI.

Royal Society. 2005. Ocean acidification due to increasing atmospheric carbon dioxide. The Royal Society, London, UK.

Vitousek, P.M. 1994. Beyond global warming: ecology and global change. Ecology 75:1861-1876.

Shea, E.L, G. Dolcemascolo, C.L. Anderson, A. Barnston, C.P. Guard, M.P. Hamnett, S.T. Kubota, N. Lewis, J. Loschnigg, and G. Meehl. 2001. Preparing for a Changing Climate: The potential Consequences of Climate Variability and Change. Published Report, East-West Center, Honolulu, HI. 100 pp.

Shun, Kanalei. 1987. Archaeological Reconnaissance Site Survey and Limited Subsurface of Baker and Howland Islands Final Report: Prepared for U.S. Army Engineer District, Honolulu Corps of Engineers, Fort Shafter, HI.

Sibley, F.C., R.B. Clapp, and C.R. Long. 1965. Biological Survey of Howland Island, March 1963–May 1965. Unpublished Report of Pacific Ocean Biological Survey Program, Division of Birds Smithsonian Institution, Washington D.C.

Skaggs, J. M. 1994. The Great Guano Rush. Entrepreneurs and American Overseas Expansion. St. Martin's Griffin, New York, NY.

Smith, S.V, and R.M. Buddemeier. 1992. Global Change and Coral Reef Ecosystems. Annual Review of Ecology and Systematics. 23:89-118.

Starbuck, A. 1878. History of the American whale fishery from its earliest inception to the year 1876. In Report of the Commissioner of Fish and Fisheries for 1875-1876. Washington, Government Printing Office. Pp. 1-779.

Townsend, C.H. 1935. The distribution of certain whales as shown by logbook records of American whaleships. Zoolologica 19:3-50.

UNESCO World Heritage Centre. 2003. Central Pacific World Heritage Project International Workshop Report, 2-6 June 2003, Honolulu, HI, USA. Paris, 44pp.

UNESCO World Heritage Centre. 2004. Central Pacific World Heritage Project, National Workshop Report, 5-11 October 2004, Kiritimati Island, the Republic of Kiribati. Paris, 11pp.

U.S. Atomic Energy Commission (USAEC). 1963. Reconnaissance Survey Report. Howland, Baker & Canton Islands. October, 1963. U.S. Atomic Energy Commission, Nevada Operations Office. Prepared by: Holmes & Narver Inc. Logistics Planning Group, Las Vegas, NV.

U.S. Fish and Wildlife Service. 1973. Baker Island, Howland Island, and Jarvis Island National Wildlife Refuges, Biological Ascertainment Reports.

U.S. Fish and Wildlife Service. 1975. Baker Island, Howland Island, and Jarvis Island National Wildlife Refuges, Narrative Report, FY 1975. Kailua, HI

U.S. Fish and Wildlife Service. 1981. Refuge Manual. Wash., D.C.

U.S. Fish and Wildlife Service. 1998a. Coral Reef Initiative in the Pacific: Howland Island, Baker Island, and Jarvis Island National Wildlife Refuges. Honolulu, HI.

U.S. Fish and Wildlife Service. 1998b. Remote islands ecosystem plan: Howland Island, Baker Island, and Jarvis Island National Wildlife Refuges. Honolulu, HI. 16 pp.

U.S. Fish and Wildlife Service. 2000. Pacific Remote Islands National Wildlife Refuge Complex Special Conditions & Rules for Moving Between Islands and Atolls and Packing for Field Camps. Honolulu, HI.

U.S. Fish and Wildlife Service. 2001. Environmental Assessment: Proposed Palmyra Atoll National Wildlife Refuge, Line Islands, Central Pacific Ocean. Portland, OR.

U.S. Fish and Wildlife Service. 2002. Birds of Conservation Concern. Arlington, VA.

U.S. Fish and Wildlife Service. 2005. Regional Seabird Conservation Plan, Pacific Region. U.S. Fish and Wildlife Service, Migratory Birds and Habitat Programs, Pacific Region, Portland, OR.

Vitousek, M.J., B. Kilonsky, and W.G. Leslie. 1980. Meteorological Observations in the Line Islands, 1972-1980. Honolulu, HI. 74 pp.

Vitousek, P.M. 1994. Beyond global warming: ecology and global change. Ecology 75:1861-1876.

Walther G.R., E. Post, P. Convey, A. Menzel, C. Parmesank, T.J.C. Beebee, J. Fromentin, O. Hoegh-GuldbergI, and F. Bairlein. 2002. Ecological responses to recent climate change. Nature 416: 389–395.

Appendix D. Planning Team Members

The following individuals were instrumental in the development of this CCP.

Name	Position	Degree(s)	Years of Exp.
Charles Pelizza*	Planning Team Leader	BA, Enviro. Science MS, Biology	26
Don Palawski*	Refuge Manager	BS, Fisheries Biology MS, Entomology	31
Bob Dieli*	Outdoor Recreation Planner	BS, Environmental Education	29
Barbara Maxfield	External Affairs Chief	BA, Business Admin/Marketing	27
Barry Stieglitz	Project Leader	BS, Forestry and Wildlife MPA, Public Admin.	18
Michael Molina	Environmental Review Coor.	BS, Biology MS, Marine Biology	30
Beth Flint*	Seabird Biologist	BS, Wildlife Biology PhD, Biology	28
LeeAnn Woodward*	Contaminant Biologist	BS, Biology MS, Ecology PhD, Ecology	30
Jim Maragos*	Coral Reef Biologist	BA, Zoology, PhD, Oceanography	38

* indicates planning team member

Appendix E. Quarantine Protocol

The following protocol was developed to maintain consistency in quarantine procedures for all NWRs in the Pacific. Thus, these provisions apply to all of the Remote Island National Wildlife Refuges. Some refuges, including Howland, may have additional restrictions and requirements.

Pacific Remote Islands National Wildlife Refuge Complex
Special Conditions and Rules for
Moving Between Islands and Atolls and
Packing for Field Camps

The islands and atolls of the Pacific Remote Islands National Wildlife Refuge Complex are special places providing habitat for many rare, endemic plants and animals. Many of these species are formally listed as federally threatened or endangered under the Endangered Species Act of 1973. Endemic plants and insects, and the predators they support, are especially vulnerable to the introduction of competing or consuming, non-native species. Such introductions may cause the extinction of island endemics, or even the destruction of entire island ecological communities. Notable local examples include: the introduction of rabbits to Laysan Island in 1902 which caused the extinction of numerous plant and insect species and 3 endemic landbird species; the introduction of rats to many Pacific Islands causing the elimination of many burrowing seabird colonies; the introduction of the annual grass, sandbur, to Laysan Island where it has out competed native bunch grass and eliminated nesting habitat for the Endangered Laysan finch; and the introduction and proliferation of numerous ant species throughout the Pacific Islands to the widespread detriment of endemic plant and insect species (refuge files).

Several of the islands within the Refuge Complex are especially pristine, and, as a result, are diverse in terms of rare and special declining native plants and animals. Nihoa Island has 13 potential candidate Endangered insect species, numerous Endangered plants, and 2 Endangered birds. Necker Island has endangered plants and 7 endemic insects that are candidates for the Endangered Species List. Laysan Island has endangered plants, five potential candidate, endangered insect species, and the Endangered Laysan finch and Laysan duck. Other islands in the Refuge Complex such as Lisianski, Howland, Baker, and Jarvis and islets in Atolls such as Rose, Pearl and Hermes Reef and French Frigate Shoals are inhabited by a variety of endemic and endangered species and require special protection from invasive species.

Other Pacific Island such as Kure and the "high islands" (Oahu, Hawaii, Maui, Kauai, etc.) as well as, certain islands within Midway Atoll, Pearl and Hermes Reef and French Frigate Shoals have native plants and/or animals that are at high risk from introduction to the relatively pristine islands discussed above. Of special concerns are introductions of non-native snakes, rats, ants and a variety of other insect and plant species. Invasive plants of highest concern are *Verbesina encelioides, Cenchrus echinatus, and Setaria verticillata.*

The U.S. Fish and Wildlife Service is responsible for the management and protection of the fish, wildlife, plants, and their habitats associated with islands of the Pacific Remote Islands NWR

Complex. No one is permitted to access any of the Refuge's islands without the express written permission of the Refuge Manager in the form of a Special Use Permit. Because of the above concerns, the following restrictions on the movement of personnel and materials to the islands of the Refuge Complex exist. Note: Kure Island and Midway Atoll are not part of this Refuge Complex.

With the exception of Tern Island, French Frigate Shoals, the following rules apply:

Clothing and Soft Gear:

- Any personnel landing boats at any island should have clean clothes and shoes, meaning that they are free of dirt and seeds.

- Any personnel going ashore at any island and moving inshore from the immediate area in which waves are breaking at the time of landing must have new footwear, new or island-specific clothes and new or island-specific soft gear that have been frozen (<4 C) for at least 48 hours.

- At the discretion of the local USFWS representative, personnel from a NOAA ship or any other vessel servicing the Refuge may be allowed on shore to visit predesignated areas for guided tours. All stipulations for clean and frozen clothes apply.

- Otherwise, any personnel entering any vegetated area, regardless of how sparse the vegetation is, must have new footwear, new clothes and new soft gear all frozen for at least 48 hours.

Definitions:

- "new" means off the shelf and never used anywhere but the island in question.
- "clothing" is all apparel , shoes, socks, over and under garments.
- "soft gear" is all gear such as daypacks, fanny packs, camera bags, camera/binocular straps, microphone covers, nets, holding or weighing bags, bedding, tents, luggage, or any fabric or material capable of harboring seeds or insects.

Clothing or gear coming off Kure and Midway should never be moved to any of the other refuge islands.

During transit, clothing and gear coming off Kure and Midway must be carefully sequestered to avoid contamination of gear bound for other remote islands. Special care must be taken to avoid contaminating gear storage areas and quarters aboard transporting vessels with seeds or insects from these islands.

General Rules:

- Regardless of origin or destination, inspect and clean all equipment, supplies, immediately prior to any trip to the Refuge. Carefully clean all clothing, footwear and soft gear following use to minimize risk of cross contamination of materials between islands.

- Pack supplies in plastic buckets with fitted lids or other sealable metal or plastic containers so they can be thoroughly cleaned inside and out. **Cardboard is not permitted on islands.** Cardboard boxes disintegrate in a short time and harbor seeds, animals, etc., which cannot be easily found or removed. **Wood is not permitted unless sealed on all surfaces.**

  Wooden boxes can also harbor insects and seeds and, therefore, are only allowed if well constructed (tight fitting seams are required). All wood must be treated, and inside and outside surfaces must be painted or varnished to provide a smooth, cleanable finish that seals all holes.

- Freeze or tarp and fumigate then seal all equipment (clothes, books, tents) immediately prior to departure. Food and cooking items need not be fumigated but should be cleaned and frozen, if freezable. Cameras, binoculars, radios, and other electronic equipment must be thoroughly cleaned, including internal inspection whenever possible, but they do not need to be frozen or fumigated. Such equipment can only be packed in wooden crates if treated as in #2 above. Any containers must contain new, clean packing materials and be frozen or fumigated.

- At present, Tern Island is the singular exception to the above rule having less stringent rules due to the large number of previously established invasive species. Careful inspection of all materials and containers is still required. However, it is acceptable to use wooden and cardboard containers for transporting supplies to Tem Island. In addition, there is no requirement for freezing or fumigating items disembarked at Tem. Although requirements for Tem Island are more lax, the Refuge is still concerned about the possibilities of new introductions.

Additional Special Conditions for Restricted Access to Nihoa Island:

Nihoa is one of the most pristine locations in the Refuge Complex. It is also inhabited by the highest number of federally listed endangered species. It is a small rugged island with many inaccessible areas. Introduction of any invasive species could have immediate, disastrous effects to natural resources. It would be almost impossible to mount any kind of control or eradication program on this island should an invasive species become established. Because of these reasons, access to Nihoa is strictly limited and rules governing entry are more stringent.

- Access to Nihoa by permittees would only be allowed under the direct supervision of a Refuge representative. The person, who shall be appointed by the Refuge Manager, would work with permittees to assure careful adherence with all rules for inspection, handling, and preparation of equipment. The Refuge Representative would have the authority to control and limit access to various parts of the island to protect animals, plants (especially endangered species), and archaeological sites. The Refuge Representative would have the authority to revoke access to the island or order an immediate departure from the island if conditions for working on the island are not fully met or are violated in some way.

- All field equipment made out of fabric material or wood must be new and never previously used in the Northwestern or main Hawaiian Islands. Equipment previously purchased or made for use on Nihoa that has been carefully sealed and stored while away from Nihoa, and not used elsewhere, may also be brought onto the island. Rules for freezing and/or fumigating are as described for other sites in the Refuge (see above).

- Clothing and personal effects must be cleaned and thoroughly inspected. All footwear (shoes, slippers, socks, etc.) must be new, unused, or previously only used on Nihoa and carefully sealed and stored while off of the island.

Rules Regarding Food:

Fresh foods that are typically transported to island field camps (potatoes, onions, cabbage, apples, oranges, etc.) are not likely to become established and flourish on the Refuge Complex and are allowed. However, other food items such as tomatoes could easily become established. Soil can contain many seeds, eggs, larvae, etc., and cannot be transported to or among islands.

Other food species such as alfalfa, mustard and cress, commonly used for sprouted greens, could potentially become established and cannot be brought to the islands. Other species such as mung beans, soybeans, and radishes would not likely survive on the islands and can be used for fresh greens. A list of fresh foods and seeds that are prohibited is provided below. Permittees should contact the Refuge Manager for more information or for questions about items not included on this list.

Strictly Prohibited:

Tomatoes (any variety), ray sunflower seeds, alfalfa seeds, mustard seeds.

Bulk dried fruits are allowed but should be frozen solid for at least one day to kill any insects.

Appendix F. Wilderness Review

I. General Information on Wilderness Reviews

Wilderness review is the process used to determine whether or not to recommend lands or waters in the National Wildlife Refuge System (System) to the United States Congress (Congress) for designation as wilderness. Planning policy for the System (602 FW 3) mandates conducting wilderness reviews every 15 years through the Comprehensive Conservation Planning (CCP) process.

The wilderness review process has three phases: inventory, study, and recommendation. After first identifying lands and waters that meet the minimum criteria for wilderness, the resulting wilderness study areas (WSA) are further evaluated to determine if they merit recommendation from the Service to the Secretary of the Interior for inclusion in the National Wilderness Preservation System (NWPS). Areas recommended for designation are managed to maintain wilderness character in accordance with management goals, objectives, and strategies outlined in the final CCP until Congress makes a decision or the CCP is amended to modify or remove the wilderness proposal. A brief discussion of wilderness inventory, study, and recommendation follows.

Wilderness Inventory: The wilderness inventory consists of identifying areas that minimally meet the requirements for of wilderness as defined in the Wilderness Act of 1964 (Wilderness Act). Wilderness is defined as an area which:
- Has at least five thousand acres of land or is of sufficient size as to make practicable its preservation and use in an unimpaired condition, or be capable of restoration to wilderness character through appropriate management at the time of review, or be a roadless island;
- Generally appears to have been affected primarily by the forces of nature, with the imprint of man's work substantially unnoticeable;
- Has outstanding opportunities for solitude or a primitive and unconfined type of recreation; and
- May also contain ecological, geological, or other features of scientific, educational, scenic, or historical value. These features and values, though desirable, are not necessary for an area to qualify as a wilderness.

Wilderness Study: During the study phase, lands and waters qualifying for wilderness as a result of the inventory are studied to analyze values (ecological, recreational, cultural, spiritual), resources (*e.g.*, wildlife, water, vegetation, minerals, soils), and uses (habitat management, public use) within the area. The findings of the study help determine whether to recommend the area for designation as wilderness.

Wilderness Recommendation: Once a wilderness study determines that a WSA meets the requirements for inclusion in the NWPS, a wilderness study report that presents the results of the wilderness review, accompanied by a Legislative Environmental Impact Statement (LEIS), is prepared. The wilderness study report and LEIS that support wilderness designation are then transmitted through the Secretary of Interior to the President of United States, and ultimately to the United States Congress for approval.

The following sections summarize the inventory and study phases of the wilderness review for Howland.

II. Wilderness Inventory

The wilderness inventory is a broad look at the planning area to identify WSAs. These WSAs are roadless areas within refuge boundaries, including submerged lands and their associated water column, that meet the minimum criteria for wilderness identified in Sect. 2(c) of the Wilderness Act. A WSA must meet the minimum size criteria (or be a roadless island), appear natural, and provide outstanding opportunities for solitude or primitive recreation. Other supplemental values are evaluated, but not required. In order to identify WSAs, Howland was divided into two inventory units based upon the differences between the terrestrial and marine ecological resources. Inventory Unit A is the 648-acre roadless island known as Howland Island, and Inventory Unit B is composed of the 34,319 combined acres of coral reefs, submergent lands and their associated water column lying within 3 nmi from the shoreline at the mean high water mark of Howland Island. The inventory of roadless areas, submerged lands, and associated water column of Howland and application of the wilderness criteria is described in the following sections and summarized in Table F-1.

Evaluation of Size Criteria for Roadless Areas, Roadless Islands, and Submergent Lands and Associated Water Column

Identification of roadless areas, roadless islands, and submerged lands and associated water column, required gathering land status maps, land use and road inventory data, satellite imagery, aerial photographs, and personal observations of areas within refuge boundaries. "Roadless" refers to the absence of improved roads suitable and maintained for public travel by means of motorized vehicles primarily intended for highway use. Wilderness inventory units currently owned by the Service in fee title were evaluated. These units include Howland Island and the submergent lands and waters lying within 3 nmi of shore.

Inventory units meet the size criteria for a WSA if any one of the following standards applies.

- An area with over 5,000 contiguous acres. State and private lands are not included in making this acreage determination.
- A roadless island of any size. A roadless island is defined as an area surrounded by permanent waters or that is markedly distinguished from the surrounding lands by topographical or ecological features.
- An area of less than 5,000 contiguous Federal acres that is of sufficient size as to make practicable its preservation and use in an unimpaired condition, and of a size suitable for wilderness management.

- An area of less than 5,000 contiguous Federal acres that is contiguous with a designated wilderness, recommended wilderness, or area under wilderness review by another Federal wilderness managing agency such as the Forest Service, National Park Service, or Bureau of Land Management.

There are no roads on Howland Island, and the submerged lands and associated water column meet the minimum acreage criteria, thus both inventory units within the refuge boundary meet one or more of the size criteria for wilderness study areas. The physical features of these units are described in detail in the Howland CCP Chapter 4.

Evaluation of the Naturalness Criteria

A WSA must meet the naturalness criteria. Section 2.(c) of the Wilderness Act defines wilderness as an area that "…generally appears to have been affected primarily by the forces of nature with the imprint of man's work substantially unnoticeable." The area must appear natural to the average visitor rather than "pristine." The presence of ecologically accurate, historic landscape conditions is not required. An area may include some man-made features and human impacts provided they are substantially unnoticeable in the unit as a whole. Human-caused hazards, such as the presence of unexploded ordnance from military activity, and the physical impacts of refuge management facilities and activities are also considered in the evaluation of the naturalness criteria. An area may not be considered unnatural in appearance solely on the basis of "sights and sounds" of human impacts and activities outside the boundary of the unit. The cumulative effects of these factors were considered in the evaluation of naturalness for each wilderness inventory unit.

In the wilderness inventory, specific man-made features and other human impacts need to be identified that affect the overall apparent naturalness of the tract. Based upon the Preferred Alternative contained in the draft CCP/EA, the following factors were primary considerations in evaluating the naturalness of the inventory units:

Historical
- abandoned crushed coral airstrip;
- Amelia Earhart day beacon (aid to navigation);
- rock cairn;
- geological monument;
- derelict airplane wing (World War II vintage); and
- abandoned well and mining activity.

Little can be seen of the historical artifacts found on Howland. The airstrip, prepared as a waypoint for Amelia Earhart's flight around the world has not been maintained since World War II. Remnants of island occupation during guano mining and World War II periods such as hand dug pits, wells and crumbled building walls are present on the island. However, wind erosion, storm activity, and vegetative growth have covered these artifacts so that they are indistinguishable from adjacent habitats on the island. The Amelia Earhart day beacon is the only visual intrusion into an otherwise natural setting.

Management Activities:
- refuge boundary sign;
- field camp;
- generators;
- control of invasive species;
- collect and stockpile marine debris;
- migratory bird surveys;
- marine surveys (including SCUBA); and
- boat transportation.

A 4'x 8' boundary sign announcing the name and ownership of the island is maintained on Howland. The sign is informational in nature, identifying the sanctuary status the island enjoys. The primary management intrusion to the naturalness of Howland is during the deployment and demobilization of field camps. Transportation from Honolulu, Hawaii across 1,600 nmi of open ocean to Howland is only safely and reliably possible with motorized ocean-going marine vessels. Once the marine transport vessel arrives at Howland, small boats with outboard motors are deployed to transport two biologists and their field camp gear to the island. Once on the island, biologists set up tents, sleeping gear, food, and other supplies. Walking surveys occur across the island to document bird species presence, potentially hand pull or hand spray invasive plant species, inventory cultural sites, and collect and stockpile marine debris. Marine surveys also occur. They are based from the marine vessel primarily using SCUBA. Field camps are planned to last for 2 days and typically occur once every two years. Occasional field camps with 5-8 individuals staying for up to 2 weeks have occurred in the past. During these extended field camps, diesel-powered generators have been used to operate communication equipment. All other mechanical equipment such as air compressors for SCUBA equipment remains on the marine transport vessel. Upon demobilization of the field camp, all equipment and debris are removed. An indirect human impact to the naturalness of Howland is the presence of marine debris that washes onto coral reefs and beaches. Attempts to remove and stockpile this debris for eventual removal occur during field camps. Otherwise, Howland is an isolated, uninhabited island in the middle of the Pacific Ocean for the vast majority of time.

Both Howland inventory units meet the naturalness criteria. Overall, the forces of nature sculpt the island's resources. Wave action erodes and accretes shorelines and rearranges underwater coral features. Rainfall patterns either suppress or encourage vegetative growth with brown and barren ground during drought and lush grasses and forbs during wet periods. Bird life is the dominant feature with nesting seabirds common throughout the year. Occasional field camps infrequently intrude on this isolation.

Although historic markers, monuments, and other signs of past human occupation exist, they do not detract from Howland meeting the naturalness criteria since they are a minor component of the landscape and are substantially unnoticeable in the area as a whole. The submerged lands, with the exception of scattered marine debris also meet the naturalness criteria.

Evaluation of Outstanding Opportunities for Solitude or Primitive and Unconfined Recreation

In addition to meeting the size and naturalness criteria, a WSA must provide outstanding opportunities for solitude or primitive recreation. The area does not have to possess outstanding opportunities for both solitude and primitive and unconfined recreation, and does not need to have outstanding opportunities on every acre. Further, an area does not have to be open to public use and access to qualify under these criteria. Congress has designated a number of wilderness areas in the NWPS that are closed to public access to protect ecological resource values.

Opportunities for solitude refer to the ability of a visitor to be alone and secluded from other visitors in the area. Primitive and unconfined recreation means non-motorized, dispersed outdoor recreation activities that do not require developed facilities or mechanical transport. These primitive recreation activities may provide opportunities to experience challenge and risk, self reliance, and adventure.

These two opportunity "elements" are not well defined by the Wilderness Act but in most cases can be expected to occur together. However, an outstanding opportunity for solitude may be present in an area offering only limited primitive recreation potential. Conversely, an area may be so attractive for recreation use that experiencing solitude is not an option.

The following factors and their cumulative effects were the primary considerations in evaluating the availability of outstanding opportunities for solitude or primitive unconfined recreation at Howland:
- island size, vegetation, and terrain;
- distance to habitation, whether mainland or an inhabited island;
- presence of operating lighthouse or aid to navigation and associated structures; and
- viewshed within and from refuge boundary.

Solitude is the overwhelming force that visitors experience on Howland. The island is separated by over 1,600 nautical miles from Hawaii, and approximately 330 nmi from Kanton Atoll, the nearest inhabited island. Expanses of open ocean with no other landform are visible from every angle. The island itself, with the exception of a few historical features, is a mixture of short grass and shrubs, bare ground, and shoreline beaches and cobble. In the past, field camps have been temporary, with only 2 individuals spending 2 days every 2 years. However, the Preferred Alternative in the Draft Howland CCP/EA proposed a visit to the refuge every year with the same number of individuals for the same duration. Underwater, coral reefs are pristine and the open-water depths are devoid of human presence.

Since establishment, Howland has been and will remain closed to general public access in order to protect the valuable seabird and marine resource values. Thus, there are no outdoor recreational opportunities.

Both Howland inventory units meet the solitude criteria, but do not meet the primitive unconfined recreation criteria.

Evaluation of Supplemental Values

Supplemental values are defined by the Wilderness Act as "ecological, geological, or other features of scientific, educational, scenic, or historic value." Howland Island and its surrounding coral reefs and deep water areas compose a complete and functioning ecosystem. Isolated, predator-free islands are valuable and often required for successful seabird nesting. Nearshore waters, coral reefs, and associated currents combine and provide food resources for foraging seabirds and coral reef communities. The position and underwater gradient of Howland in deep ocean currents allows these currents to reach the surface, thereby increasing rates of productivity for plants, corals and vertebrate species. These rich ecological resources in a relatively pristine and unaltered environment provide unique opportunities for scientific study and environmental education. There are no known archaeological resources on Howland. Historically, Howland Island was important to early colonization efforts during the guano mining era, and as the ill-fated destination for Amelia Earhart and Fred Noonan on their around the world flight. Historical artifacts such as isolated building ruins, an abandoned runway, and guano mining excavations are present but eroded, covered by vegetation, and otherwise assimilated into the environment and indistinguishable from the natural environment. One historical landmark, the Amelia Earhart day beacon, contrasts vividly with the overall expansive vistas of open ocean and island habitats. These values are not required for wilderness but their presence compliments the requirements for wilderness designation. Please see Chapter 4 of the CCP/EA for a more complete description of these supplemental values.

Inventory Findings and Wilderness Study Areas

Both inventory units meet the minimum criteria for consideration as WSAs (Figure F-1). These two units are either roadless islands or meet minimum size requirements, are primarily natural, and meet the solitude or unconfined recreation criteria. The units are identified as:

- WSA-A: Howland Island WSA, and
- WSA-B: Coral reefs, submergent lands, and associated water column of the Howland Island WSA.

Figure F-1. Wilderness Study Areas

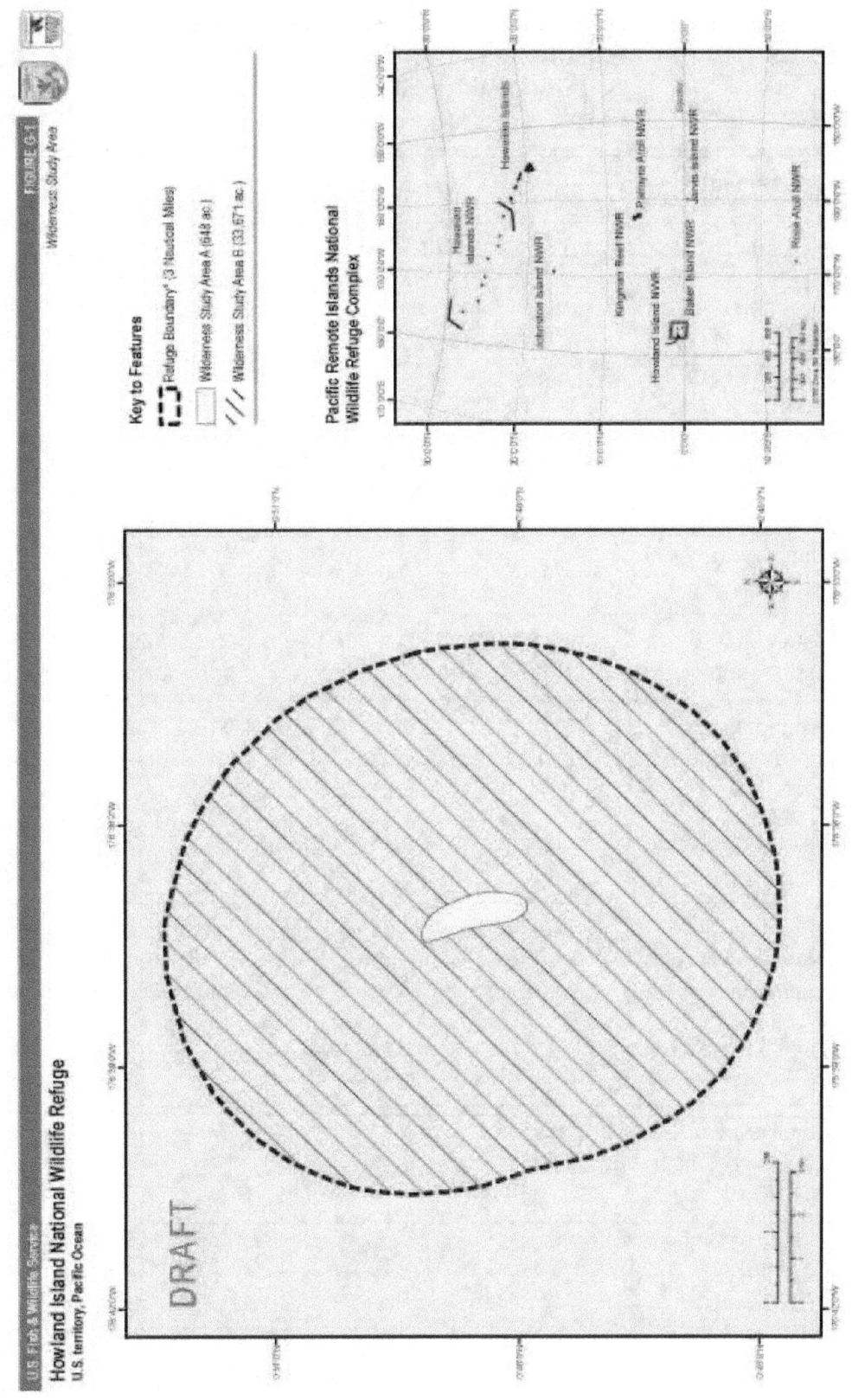

Table F-1 Wilderness Inventory Summary

	Inventory Unit A: Howland Island (330 acres)	Inventory Unit B: Submerged lands and waters to 3 nmi (34,000 acres)
Required Components		
(1) Has at least 5000 acres of land or is of sufficient size to make practicable its preservation and use in an unconfined condition, or is a roadless island.	Yes. Is a roadless island.	Yes. Approximately 34,000 acres contained within the territorial sea from mean high tide to 3 nmi.
(2) Generally appears to have been affected primarily by the forces of nature, with the imprint of man's work substantially unnoticeable.	Yes. Not diminished by day beacon and other artifacts.	Yes. Coral reefs and other underwater features untouched by humans.
(3a) Has outstanding opportunities for solitude.	Yes. Uninhabited island 1000 nmi from Hawaii.	Yes. Isolation from habitation both on surface and below.
(3b) Has outstanding opportunities for a primitive and unconfined type of recreation.	No. Refuge is closed to all recreational activities.	No. Refuge is closed to all recreational activities.
Other Components		
(4) Contains ecological, geological or other features of scientific, educational, scenic, or historical value.	Earhart day beacon, WWII artifacts, guano mining, and nesting seabirds.	Pristine coral reefs and associated marine fish, mammals, and turtles abound.
Summary		
Parcel qualifies as a wilderness study area (meets criteria 1, 2 & 3a or 3b).	Yes	Yes

III. Wilderness Study

The two WSAs identified in the Wilderness Inventory were further evaluated to determine suitability for designation, management, and preservation as wilderness. Considerations in this evaluation included:

- quality of wilderness values; and,
- capability for management of refuge as wilderness (or manageability) and minimum requirements/tools analysis.

This information provides a basis to compare the impacts of a range of management alternatives and determine the most appropriate management direction for each WSA.

Evaluation of Wilderness Values

The following information considers the quality of the WSAs' mandatory and supplemental wilderness characteristics.

Size

Both WSA-A and WSA-B meet the minimum size criteria being a 648-acre roadless island and a 34,319-acre marine ecosystem respectively.

Naturalness

Both of the WSAs generally appear to have been affected primarily by the forces of nature, with the imprint of human uses and activities substantially unnoticeable. Except for the footprint of the long-abandoned airstrip and the few small features mentioned in the Wilderness Inventory, all emergent and submerged features were entirely created by the natural processes of volcanism; wind erosion; wave erosion; water erosion; seabird deposits; vegetation deposits; geological subsidence; and reef growth and consolidation from coral, coralline algae, and giant clam calcification during the past 50 to 80 million years. No substantial features were constructed or modified by humans during the island's entire geological history. The impacts of past human presence are small in terms of constructed features (beacons, monuments), and are barely apparent (ground-level views of the airfield, mining pits, boat channel), or transitory (marine debris that washes up or blows in from the surrounding sea and air). A few remnant, rusty fuel drums is the only trash feature that is not transient, but its overall impact to naturalness is minimal. See Chapter 4 of the Howland CCP/EA for a more detailed description of natural and cultural features. Management activities will temporarily disturb the naturalness of the area. Field camps lasting for 2 days will be visible across the island. Occasional use of generators will produce noise. However, modern generators produce decibel levels lower than speaking voice levels. Transportation by motorized marine vessel, the only safe, practical and reliable means available to arrive on the island, is equally temporary.

Outstanding Opportunities for Solitude and Primitive Recreation

Both of the WSAs offer outstanding opportunities for solitude.

Solitude overwhelms the human spirit at Howland. The only noise on the island is from pounding surf, winds, buzzing insects, and the calls of birds. Underwater, all that is heard is one's own breath, the surf, and the sound of fish feeding on coral. The blue of the sky and sea and the brightness of the stark landscape saturate the visual character; and birds, winds, and surf saturate the acoustic character of the refuge. It is hard to image a more remote, isolated, and truly more wilderness experience in the entire equatorial Pacific than when standing on the island or diving on adjacent reefs.

There are no permanent improvements of any kind to accommodate visitors reaching the island. The capacity to reach Howland without substantial investment, preplanning, and permission is considerable and further restricts the capability of individuals from reaching the island and intruding on the opportunity for solitude. The island itself is inaccessible except by small craft lightered from a transport ship during calm seas. The airstrip is unusable and has never been maintained since World War II. Island vegetation, erosion, and accretion have reclaimed the airstrip and now make it unrecognizable. There are no human inhabitants on Howland. The nearest humans live 330 nmi to the southeast where less than 100 Kiribati people inhabit Kanton Atoll. There are no other inhabitants elsewhere in the Phoenix Islands. These logistical constraints contribute to the maintenance of solitude.

Supplemental Values

Both of the WSAs offer outstanding ecological values with features of scientific, educational, scenic interest, and historical value. Pristine coral reefs, reef fish, giant clams, beaches, native terrestrial vegetation, unexplored deep slopes, localized upwelling currents, migratory shorebirds, and large populations and variety of seabirds are among the strong ecological values. The lack of historic and current human impact provides a rare opportunity to study unaltered marine ecosystems, and the impact that global climate change may have on these systems. The sheer vastness of the ocean landscape, punctuated by a small dot of land, and the multitude of bird and marine life attracted to it, provide a sense of awe and spectacular beauty to the landscape. The remaining features of early colonization efforts, as well as the memorial to Amelia Earhart, stand testament to the bravery of those early pioneers, and the ability of nature to endure.

Evaluation of Manageability and Minimum Requirements/Tools Analysis

Originally administered by the U.S. Department of Interior's Office of Territorial Affairs, the Secretary of the Interior (Secretary), on June 27, 1974, designated Howland Island and its territorial sea extending to the 3 nautical mile (nmi) limit as a unit of the System (39 FR 27930). The U.S. Fish and Wildlife Service administers all units of the system pursuant to the Administration Act. The acquisition authority for establishing the refuge is found in the Fish and Wildlife Act of 1956 (16 U.S.C. 742f(b)(1)). It states the general purpose for establishing the refuge is "...for the development, advancement, management, conservation, and protection of fish and wildlife resources..." and "...for the benefit of the United States Fish and Wildlife Service, in performing its activities and services" (16 U.S.C. 742f (a) (4)). The specific purpose for establishing Howland is (USFWS 1973): "...the restoration and preservation of the complete ecosystem, terrestrial and marine. Special consideration must be given to the protection of nesting seabird populations." There are no valid existing private rights, including mineral rights, associated with any of these WSAs.

Several management activities are required for the Service to meet responsibilities for managing Howland Island and its associated marine waters as a national wildlife refuge as specified in relevant legislation and policies. A complete description of management activities can be found in Chapter 2 of the Howland CCP/EA. The following is a brief description of management activities as they relate to minimum requirement determinations of activities occurring within designated wilderness.

Section 4(c) of the Wilderness Act of 1964 lists several generally prohibited uses including no temporary roads, no use of motor vehicles, no motorized equipment or motorboats, no aircraft landings, no other forms of mechanical transport, and no structure or installation. However, Section 4(c) also states an exception to these general prohibitions: "...as necessary to meet minimum requirements for the administration of the area for the purpose of this Act..." Examples of actions that may satisfy this exception include recreational developments such as trails, bridges, and signs.

Each WSA on Howland can be managed to preserve its wilderness character in perpetuity, recognizing that using a "minimum requirements" approach would be required for all activities. Existing refuge management activities within the WSAs are consistent with management direction in the Wilderness Act and current Service wilderness stewardship policy in the Refuge Manual (6 RM 8). These management activities include: motorized marine vessel transportation to and from Howland; establishing temporary field camps (typically 2 days every other year); small motorboat operations used in deployment and demobilization of field camp operations; survey and monitoring of habitat, seabird and other wildlife monitoring activities; control of invasive species using hand pulling or hand spraying; use of solar powered electronic calling devices to encourage nesting by extirpated seabird species; use of portable generators and solar power to operate communications and other equipment; and monitoring the marine ecosystem with the use of SCUBA equipment. None of the current or expected refuge management activities would permanently diminish the wilderness character of Howland. Additionally, there are no plans to construct permanent facilities or structures to accommodate these uses or activities.

Located in the central Pacific Ocean, transportation to Howland can only occur with the use of ocean-going marine vessels. The only practical and safe mode of vessel propulsion is gas or diesel powered engine. While it is possible to use sail power to navigate to the island, the reliability of mechanical engines provides a margin of safety to escape extreme weather hazards, or proceed on course and on time in the absence of wind. For the same reasons of safety and practicality, small motorized vessels are used to transport equipment and personnel from the transport vessel to the island to establish field camps and conduct biological survey and monitoring activities. Rough surf, shallow coral reefs, and strong winds preclude the use of non-motorized craft to safely navigate these hazards.

Field camps themselves are temporary, consisting of tents, portable tables, chairs, cooking gear, and scientific equipment. Most field camps are set up for a period of 1 to 2 days. No permanent structures are established, and no motorized equipment is used to transport equipment around the island. Field camp activities consist of monitoring habitat and nesting seabird populations, inventorying the condition of known historic resources, and collecting and stockpiling of marine debris. Portable diesel powered generators are components of field camp equipment and are typically used to operate two-way radio communication equipment.

Wildlife managers often use electronic calling devices to attract nesting seabird species to suitable nesting locations. Powered by small solar panels, these devices can be placed in inconspicuous locations and produce only sounds that occur naturally on the island. Once a species is attracted to the island, the calling devise can then be removed. Monitoring of the marine ecosystem occurs from scientists based aboard the marine transportation vessel. Small motorboats often provide safe transportation to specific research sites near Howland. SCUBA equipment is often used to complete marine surveys and is the only safe and practical method of conducting underwater marine surveys.

In summary, safety, practicality, and effectiveness require the occasional use of management programs and associated tools (some of which are generally prohibited by the Wilderness Act) to pursue achievement of refuge purposes, goals and objectives. Current and proposed refuge management would be consistent with wilderness designation and management of both WSAs. Although occasionally diminished, none of the resource values identified above would be permanently impacted because of wilderness designation and the management described herein.

IV. Development of Alternatives

After evaluating the quality of wilderness values, manageability, minimum management requirements, the following alternatives were developed and analyzed for wilderness designation.

> Alternative A (No Action).
> Under this alternative, no WSAs would be recommended as suitable for wilderness designation. The refuge lands and waters would be managed as they have been in the past to accomplish refuge purposes in accordance with legal and policy guidance for the System.

> Alternative B
> Only the emergent lands, WSA-A, would be recommended for inclusion in the National Wilderness Preservation System.

> Alternative C
> Both WSA-A and WSA-B, which includes the emergent lands and the submerged lands and associated water column would be immediately recommended for inclusion in the

National Wilderness Preservation System (NWPS). Selection of this alternative would require the completion of an EIS.

<u>Alternative D (Preferred Alternative)</u>
Both WSA-A and WSA-B, which includes the emergent lands and the submerged lands and associated water column of Howland would be recommended for inclusion in the NWPS. Both wilderness study areas would be managed to ensure their wilderness character was not adversely impacted. However, the recommendation to include these areas in the NWPS would be postponed until such time that CCPs and their associated wilderness inventories and studies for remote Pacific Island NWRs were completed. At such a time, a wilderness study report and associated Legislative Environmental Impact Statement that encompasses remote Pacific Island refuges would be prepared. Alternative D is identified here as the Preferred Alternative for the Wilderness Review of Howland, and is a component of the Preferred Alternative in the Draft Howland CCP/EA.

<u>Alternatives considered but eliminated from detailed study</u>

Federal agencies are required by NEPA to rigorously explore and objectively evaluate all reasonable alternatives and to briefly discuss the reasons for eliminating any alternatives that were not developed in detail (40 CFR 1502.14). It was determined that there was no benefit in analyzing partial wilderness alternatives. There are no feasible or practical boundary adjustments that would improve the manageability of an individual WSA.

Appendix G. Statement of Compliance

STATEMENT OF COMPLIANCE
for Implementation of the
Howland Island National Wildlife Refuge
Comprehensive Conservation Plan

The following executive orders and legislative acts have been reviewed as they apply to implementation of the Comprehensive Conservation Plan (CCP) for the Howland Island National Wildlife Refuge (Howland).

National Environmental Policy Act (1969) (42 U.S.C. 4321 et seq.). The CCP planning process has been conducted in accordance with National Environmental Policy Act implementing procedures, Department of the Interior and Service procedures, and is performed in coordination with the affected public. Procedures used to reach this decision meet the requirements of the National Environmental Policy Act and its implementing regulations in 40 CFR Parts 1500-1508. These procedures include: the development of a range of alternatives for the Howland CCP; analysis of the likely effects of each alternative; and public involvement throughout the planning process.

The CCP management objectives and alternatives have been integrated into an environmental assessment document and process, including the release of a Draft CCP/EA for a 30-day public comment period. Public notices of availability of the Draft CCP/EA include a Federal Register notice, news releases to local media outlets, the Service's refuge planning website, and planning updates. Copies of the Draft CCP/EA and planning updates were distributed to an extensive mailing list. In addition, the Service met with staff from the Hawaii Department of Land and Natural Resources and the National Oceanic and Atmospheric Administration. Revisions to the final CCP are based on public comments received on the Draft CCP/EA. Comment letters and Service response to comments can be found as an Appendix in the CCP.

National Historic Preservation Act (1966) (16 U.S. C.470 et seq.). This act requires Federal agencies to consult with the President's Advisory Council on Historic Preservation (ACHP), State or Territorial Historic Preservation Officers, and the National Park Service (NPS) for any proposed actions that may affect cultural resources eligible for the National Register of Historic Places. Consultation has occurred with the ACHP and NPS for their input. Consultation with a State Historic Preservation Officer is not required for this proposal because Howland lies outside any state jurisdiction. No Territorial Historic Preservation Officer is assigned to Howland. Rather territories/possessions lie in the jurisdiction of the Advisory Council on Historic Preservation (ACHP).

The management of archaeological and cultural resources of Howland complies with the regulations of Section 106 of the National Historic Preservation Act. No historic properties listed in or eligible for listing in the National Register of Historic Places have been identified on Howland. No historic properties are known to be affected by the proposed action based on the criteria of an effect or adverse effect as an undertaking defined in 36 CFR 800.9 and Service Manual 614 FW 2. Determining whether a particular action has a potential to affect cultural resources is an ongoing process that occurs as step-down and site-specific project plans are developed. Should historic properties be identified in the future, the Service will comply with the National Historic Preservation Act if any management actions have the potential to affect any these properties.

Comprehensive Environmental Response, Compensation, and Liability Act (CERCLA), Secretarial Order 3127, and Section 211 of the Superfund Amendments and Reauthorization Act (SARA) of 1986 (10 U.S.C. 2701-2706, 2810-2811). Contamination resulting from military occupation is required to be mitigated as a Formerly Used Defense Site (FUDS). Any FUDS is part of the Defense Environmental Restoration Program (DERP), administered by the Army Corps of Engineers (ACOE). The DERP is responsible for the identification, investigation, research and development, and cleanup of contamination from hazardous substances, and pollutants and contaminants; correction of environmental damage such as detection and disposal of unexploded ordnance; and demolition and removal of unsafe buildings and structures at former Department of Defense sites. In 1986, the ACOE completed their responsibilities under DERP. No contaminant or hazardous waste materials are currently known to exist on Howland.

Executive Order 13175. Consultation and Coordination with Indian Tribal Governments. As required under Secretary of the Interior Order 3206 American Indian Tribal Rights, Federal-Tribal Responsibilities, and the Endangered Species Act, the Refuge Manager determined that there are no tribal governments associated with Howland. Thus, there was no coordination with any American Indian tribe.

Executive Order 12372. Intergovernmental Review. Coordination and consultation with other affected Federal agencies has been completed through personal contact by Service planners, refuge managers, and supervisors. In addition, the refuge manager determined there are no local, state or tribal governments associated with Howland.

Executive Order 12898. Federal Actions to Address Environmental Justice in Minority and Low-Income Populations. All Federal actions must address and identify, as appropriate, disproportionately high and adverse human health or environmental effects of its programs, policies, and activities on minority populations, low-income populations, and Indian Tribes in the United States. The CCP was evaluated and no adverse human health or environmental effects were identified for minority or low-income populations, Indian Tribes, or anyone else.

Migratory Bird Treaty Act (MBTA)(16 U.S.C. 703-712) Howland is an important site for migratory shorebirds and nesting seabirds. Protecting nesting seabird habitat is the major purpose of the refuge, and is consistent with the provisions of MBTA. All of the proposed alternatives would be consistent with the refuge purpose and the MBTA in protecting these birds. The proposed action, however, would afford more benefits. This planning effort is being coordinated with other offices of the Service and Interior that have responsibilities pertaining to the MBTA.

Executive Order 13186. Responsibilities of Federal Agencies to Protect Migratory Birds. This Order directs departments and agencies to take certain actions to further implement the Migratory Bird Treaty Act. A provision of the Order directs Federal agencies to consider the impacts of their activities, especially in reference to birds on the Fish and Wildlife Service's list of Birds of Conservation (Management) Concern (BCC). It also directs agencies to incorporate conservation recommendations and objectives found within the North American Waterbird Conservation Plan and bird conservation plans developed by Partners in Flight (PIF) into agency planning. Species selected as focal conservation targets in the CCP were identified from multiple sources including pertinent BCC lists, applicable Flyway Management Plans, and regional seabird and shorebird conservation plans. The effects of all alternatives on focal conservation targets were assessed during this planning process.

Endangered Species Act (ESA) (16 U.S.C. 1531-1544). The ESA provides for the conservation of threatened and endangered species of fish, wildlife, and plants by Federal action and by encouraging the establishment of state programs. It provides for the determination and listing of endangered and threatened species and the designation of critical habitats. Section 7 of the ESA requires refuge managers to perform consultation before initiating projects that affect or may affect endangered species.

Howland provides feeding and potentially nesting habitats for two species of endangered sea turtle: the hawksbill turtle, *Eretmochelys imbricata* and the green turtle *Chelonia mydas*. In accordance with section 7 of the Endangered Species Act of 1973, as amended (16 U.S.C. 1531 et. Seq.), the Service, as a component of this CCP/EA, evaluated potential impacts to the two listed turtle species. It was determined that undertaking any action as part of any alternative in this CCP will have no affect on either of the two turtle species. Therefore, formal consultation with NOAA-NMFS is not required and will not be initiated.

National Wildlife Administration Act of 1966, as amended by The National Wildlife Refuge System Improvement Act of 1997 (16 U.S.C. 668dd-668ee). The National Wildlife Refuge System Improvement Act requires the Service to develop and implement a comprehensive conservation plan for each refuge. These conservation plans identify and describe a refuge purpose; refuge vision and goals; fish, wildlife, and plant populations and related habitats; archaeological and cultural values of the refuge; issues that may affect populations and habitats of fish, wildlife, and plants; actions necessary to restore and improve biological diversity of the refuge; and opportunities for wildlife-dependent recreation.

Wilderness Preservation Act of 1964 (Wilderness Act). The Wilderness Act requires the Service to evaluate the suitability of Howland for wilderness designation (Appendix F) and has found that both wilderness study areas meet wilderness criteria. Recommendation for Howland to be included in the Wilderness Preservation System is deferred until such time that other remote Pacific island refuges are evaluated for wilderness designation and a combined proposal as part of a larger comprehensive Legislative Environmental Impact Statement is prepared.

Magnuson-Stevens Fisheries Management and Conservation Act (16 U.S.C. 1801-1882).
This act provides the guidance for sustainable management of commercial fisheries in
Federal waters by NOAA in consultation with Regional Fisheries Management Councils that
develop fisheries management plans (FMPS) subject to NOAA approval, monitoring and
implementation. The Western Pacific Regional Fisheries Management Council (WESPAC)
and NOAA have implemented and approved several FMPS that apply to U.S. insular Pacific
island waters. The FMPS were all implemented after Howland was established in 1974 and
include plans for: 1) pelagic fish; 2) bottom fish including some reef species; 3) crustaceans
including lobsters; 4) precious corals and; 5) coral reef ecosystem species. Commercial
activities including commercial fishing are prohibited in surrounding marine water and
benthic habitat out to the 3 nmi limit because Howland Island is established as a National
Wildlife Refuge that is closed to public uses. Moreover, the Service retains jurisdiction and
management for any fisheries within the refuge. Available information indicates commercial
fishing under the auspices of any of the FMPS is not and cannot be pursued within the 3 nmi
boundary of the refuge. In addition, the Magnuson-Stevens Fisheries Management and
Conservation Act jurisdiction is subject to other applicable laws and does not apply in
Howland Island National Wildlife Refuge because this area is closed to public access and
commercial fishing under the existing National Wildlife Refuge System Administration Act,
as amended (16 U.S.C.668dd -6688ee).

Executive Order 13089, Coral Reef Protection (June 11, 1998). The purpose of this
Executive order is "…to preserve and protect the biodiversity, health, heritage, and social and
economic value of U.S. coral reef ecosystems and the marine environment..." It directs all
Federal agencies to identify actions that may affect U.S. coral reefs; utilize their programs
and authorities to protect and enhance coral reef ecosystems; and assure their actions would
not degrade those ecosystems. Federal agencies whose actions affect U.S. coral reef
ecosystems are further directed to implement measures needed to research, monitor, manage,
and restore affected ecosystems, including, but not limited to, measures reducing impacts
from pollution, sedimentation, and fishing. This Executive Order also initially established
the U.S. Coral Reef Task Force, co-chaired by the Secretaries of the Interior and Commerce,
through the Administrator of NOAA. The Task Force has oversight responsibility for
implementation of policy and Federal agency responsibilities found in this order, and support
activities under the U.S. Coral Reef Initiative. In addition, this order directs the Task Force
to work cooperatively with State, territory, commonwealth, and local government partners to
map, monitor, conserve, mitigate, and restore coral reef ecosystems.

The Proposed Action and other alternatives are fully consistent with the spirit and intent of
the Executive order. Copies of the Draft and final CCP/EA were provided to the Directorate
of the Coral Reef Task Force for coordination.

**Coral Reef Conservation Act and Executive Order 13158, Marine Protected Areas (16
U.S.C. 6401-6409) (May 26, 2000).** These statutes collectively direct Federal agencies to
coordinate among themselves and State and Territorial governments via the Coral Reef Task
Force to protect and enhance coral reefs and avoid actions that degrade reefs, promote marine
protected area development and reef restoration, and provide conservation grants and
cooperative agreements (including States and institutions) to conduct research and

development of existing and candidate marine protected areas located on coral reefs. The Coral Reef Conservation Act of 2000 is scheduled for reauthorization in 2007.

The Proposed Action and other alternatives are consistent with the spirit and intent of these policies. Howland is one of only a few Federal no-take marine protected areas in the equatorial Pacific. Implementation of the Proposed Action would materially improve surveillance and enforcement and discourage unauthorized take of fish and wildlife within the refuge and improve the capacity of the Service to monitor fish and wildlife and manage their protection within the refuge.

_____   9/16/08
Chief, Division of Planning and Visitor Services   Date

Appendix H. Plan Implementation and Costs

Introduction

Following public review and comment, public notification of the Service's decision, and CCP approval, Refuge staff will implement the CCP. This appendix describes the various partnerships, management plans, staffing and projects required to implement the plan over the next 15 years.

Staffing

The proportion of current staffing and proposed staffing within the Pacific Remote Islands NWR Complex dedicated to Howland are shown in the following tables. The proposed staffing indicates a 0.16 full-time-equivalent increase over current levels. This represents the difference in staffing needs from visiting Howland once every other year to once every year.

Current Staffing for Howland Island NWR

Staff	Employment Status and Proportion of Time[1]	Salary Rating
Project Leader	PFT (0.01 FTE)	GS 13
Supervisory Wildlife Biologist	PFT (0.07 FTE)	GS 12
Coral Reef Biologist	PFT (0.07 FTE)	GS 12
Administrative Officer	PFT (0.01 FTE)	GS 9

[1] PFT = Permanent Full Time; FTE = Full Time Equivalent where 1.0 equals one staff year.

Proposed Staffing for Howland Island NWR

Staff	Employment Status and Proportion of Time[1]	Salary Rating
Project Leader	PFT (0.02 FTE)	GS 13
Supervisory Wildlife Biologist	PFT (0.14 FTE)	GS 12
Coral Reef Biologist	PFT (0.14 FTE)	GS 12
Administrative Officer	PFT (0.02 FTE)	GS 9

[1] PFT = Permanent Full Time; FTE = Full Time Equivalent where 1.0 equals one staff year.

Funding

The following table describes the estimated annual cost to implement the CCP.

Field Camp Budget for Howland	Cost
Staff	$34,000 (0.3 FTE per year)
Supplies	$7,000
Remote Sensing equipment	N/A
Remote Sensing operations	N/A
Deep sea exploration	$25,000 per submersible vessel dive
Seabird recolonization initiative	$10,000
Vessel Charter	N/A
Vessel Purchase (one time cost)	N/A
Vessel operation	N/A
Adjusted annual personnel and operating costs	$76,000/yr

Projects

The table below contains projects developed as part of the Refuge Operating Needs System (RONS) and Service Asset Maintenance Management System (SAMMS). Brief project descriptions and their associated costs are provided. Funding of these projects would assist refuge staff in achieving the goals, objectives, and strategies of the CCP for Howland Island NWR.

Projects: RONS and SAMMS List

Project No.	Title and Description	Cost Estimate (Thousands)	Station Rank
97003	**Inventory and Monitor Terrestrial Resources:** Provide a wildlife biologist to inventory and monitor terrestrial plants, invertebrates and nesting seabirds. Remote Pacific Islands provide the only secure habitat for nesting seabirds, sea turtles and marine life within thousands of square miles of ocean.	325.25	9
00001	**Eliminate Exotic Rodent Species on Remote Pacific Islands:** Provide biological technicians and transportation expenses to restore habitat for pelagic seabirds and terrestrial plant and animal species on Howland, Baker and Jarvis NWRs.	194.0	10
980002	**Eliminate Exotic Rodent Species on Remote Pacific Islands:** Provide Wildlife Refuge Specialist to supervise biological technicians and transportation expenses to restore habitat for pelagic seabirds and terrestrial plant/ animal species on Howland, Baker and Jarvis NWRs.	174.75	10

Project No.	Title and Description	Cost Estimate (Thousands)	Station Rank
00002	**Develop interpretative program, Remote Island NWRs:** Develop a brochure for Baker, Howland and Jarvis Island NWRs and host 3 special outreach events every year in Hawaii.	23.9	999
00006	**Staff and maintain a new vessel to accomplish basic refuge operations:** This vessel would provide basic logistical support for 16 islands and remote field stations on nine different national wildlife refuges across the Pacific Ocean. The vessel would be similar in size and capability to the M/V Tiglax at Alaska Maritime NWR.	204.8	3
00018	**Inventory and monitor coral reef resources:** Remote refuges contain some of the most valuable and spectacular marine and coralline resources in the National Wildlife Refuge System. Howland Island NWR is so remote that basic knowledge of marine resources is lacking. There is a need to perform biennial monitoring of the marine resources at this refuge.	137.0	4
98004	**Install remote surveillance system:** Acquire camera equipment and service contract with a satellite communications provider to detect incursion by unauthorized visitors, such as poachers and commercial fishing vessels to assist the Coast Guard and Refuge Law Enforcement Officers in investigating illegal activities within the Refuge.	241.2	14
90100411	**Replace broken, rotten, and vandalized signs:** Replace degraded entrance signs to deter trespass and prevent introduction of invasive species.	190.0	6
02121745	**Rehabilitate historic Amelia Earhart Day Beacon:** This beacon not only has historic significance, it is also used as a landmark by mariners. The beacon requires structural repairs and painting.	355.0	999

Partnerships

Partnerships are an important component of implementation of the Howland Island NWR CCP. Refuge staff would strengthen existing partnerships with the U.S. Coast Guard, the National Oceanic and Atmospheric Administration, and the University of Hawaii Undersea Research Laboratory to implement enhanced law enforcement coverage at this remote location and facilitate inventory and monitoring of marine resources. In addition, the refuge staff would seek to enhance its volunteer program. Volunteers are critically important in providing the logistical support in the Honolulu office and field support required to effectively manage and operate year-round field camps at remote locations.

Step-Down Management Plans

The CCP is one of several plans necessary for refuge management. The CCP provides guidance in the form of goals, objectives, and strategies for several refuge program areas but may lack some of the specifics need for implementation. Given the abbreviated and qualitative once-a-year management activities identified in the preferred alternative, step-down plans would not be developed for individual program areas after CCP completion. The Draft Seabird Monitoring Assessment for Hawaii and the Pacific Islands (Citta and Reynolds, 2006), U.S. Pacific Islands Regional Shorebird Conservation Plan, Seabird Conservation Plan for the Pacific Region, and U.S. Coral Reef Task Force planning efforts would be applied to refuge operations described in the preferred alternative.

Appendix I. Consultation and Coordination

This section describes consultation and coordination efforts with the public, interested groups, and other agencies through the draft CCP/EA phase. Public involvement was sought throughout the planning process using meetings, newsletters, and other communication tools. All comments and responses to comments on the draft CCP may be found in Appendix J.

<u>Planning Updates</u>

The first Planning Update was mailed to 249 private individuals; nongovernmental organizations; local, state, Federal and international governments; and members of the media throughout the Pacific on October 12, 2005. The comment period identified in the Planning Update closed on November 14, 2005. This update announced the intent of the Service to produce a CCP for Howland, and invited comments on issues and concerns and interest in attending public meetings. A total of five responses were received.

A second planning update was mailed on May 17, 2006. This update announced the development of a list of alternatives and solicited comments on the draft alternatives. This update was mailed to 253 private individuals; non-governmental organizations; local, state, Federal and international governments; and members of the media throughout the Pacific.

A third Planning Update was mailed with the Draft Howland Island Comprehensive Conservation Plan and Environmental Assessment in September 2007. This Planning Update and the Draft CCP/EA was distributed to about 190 individuals and organizations, and posted on Region 1's website. Nine review comments were received during the 45-day comment period.

<u>Agency and Interest Group Consultation/Coordination</u>

Members of the planning team met with NOAA staff and the Hawaii Department of Land and Natural Resources (DLNR) on May 31, 2005. Refuge staff also met with members of The Nature Conservancy on June 2, 2005. Both NOAA and DLNR informally indicated that they were interested in the process, wished to be kept informed of planning progress and would review the draft plan when it became available.

A second meeting between State, NOAA, and Service staff was held on May 19, 2006 to discuss issues of mutual interest, which included their potential involvement in the Service's CCP process. A follow-up formal request was sent to the agencies on June 7, 2006.

Howland Island is uninhabited and an unincorporated U.S. territory far removed and beyond the jurisdiction of any State, insular area, or foreign nation. Other parties involved in correspondence related to this document included multiple nongovernmental organizations, U.S. Environmental Protection Agency; National Park Service; U.S. Geological Survey; U.S. Department of Defense; President's Advisory Council on Historic Preservation; National Oceanic and Atmospheric Administration (NOAA); Western Pacific Regional Fishery

Management Council; Hawaii Department of Land and Natural Resources; Hawaii Office of Hawaiian Affairs; Governor of Hawaii; the Honorary Consulate-General of the Republic of Kiribati; and the United Nations Educational, Scientific and Cultural Organization (UNESCO).

Federal Register Notices

The Notice of Intent to prepare a CCP for these refuges was published in the Federal Register on September 14, 2005.

The Notice of Availability of the Draft Howland Island Comprehensive Conservation Plan and Environmental Assessment was published in the Federal Register on September 18, 2007.

Appendix J. Response to Comments

The Refuge received four letters and five emails in response to the Draft CCP/EA. Comments are summarized below by topic. The comment is either quoted directly or paraphrased based upon the comment received.

1. Wildlife Management

Comment: We encourage the Service to maintain its "wildlife first" philosophy and to prescribe the best and most thorough protection for plants and animals. (The Wilderness Society)

Service Response: By implementing the preferred alternative Howland Island NWR will continue to be managed as a wild, natural area. This management regime will contribute to the recovery, protection, and management efforts for all native species with special consideration for seabirds, migratory shorebirds, federally listed threatened and endangered species, and coral reef species.

Comment: We recommend that an effort to inventory, monitor, protect and enhance habitat for refuge species is outlined in the CCP. (The Wilderness Society)

Service Response: The CCP contains specific objectives and strategies to inventory, monitor, protect, and enhance native terrestrial habitats and marine communities that are representative of remote tropical Pacific Islands.

Comment: It is not clear what the scientific basis is for the statement linking seabird health to pelagic fisheries in the equatorial waters surrounding the three islands. NMFS requests the FWS to provide NMFS and the Western Pacific Regional Fisheries Management Council more information, including scientific support for that statement. (National Marine Fisheries Service)

Service Response: Information and scientific citations have been added to the plan to document the linkage between pelagic fish activity and its importance to seabird foraging activity.

Comment: The CCP should include a method to inventory the impact of human activities on species populations. (The Wilderness Society)

Service Response: Refuge management will be limited to monitoring terrestrial and marine plants and animals and removal of non-native species. The Refuges will also remain closed to public use to protect the extensive seabird nesting colonies, reduce the threat of introduction of invasive species, and conserve the pristine coral reef ecosystems. So the low level of human activities will have non-detectable impacts species populations.

Comment: The Final CCPs should include monitoring and enforcement provisions. (Marine Conservation Biology Institute)

Service Response: We agree. Goal 5 of the CCP has been expanded to include biological resource preservation. An objective and associated strategy has been added to encompass enforcement provisions to accomplish the preservation goal.

Comment: I highly recommend consultation with NMFS and our partners before any proposal for fisheries enforcement activities. (National Marine Fisheries Service)

Service Response: We agree with this recommendation and look forward to continuing the existing collaborative relationship that exists among our respective agency's law enforcement personnel.

Comment: We request that the Service analyze and disclose all wildlife and fisheries management and conservation plans in the CCP. (The Wilderness Society)

Service Response: Regional and Ecosystem Conservation Plans important for developing the CCP are summarized in Section 1.4.5 of the plan.

Comment: The CCP and preferred alternative B do not meet the mission of the National Wildlife Refuge System. (Center for Biological Diversity)

Service Response: We respectfully disagree. The goals and their respective strategies and activities in the CCP are designed to manage for "wildlife first" at Howland Island NWR and contribute to the System's national network of lands and waters administered for "the conservation, management and where appropriate, restoration of fish, wildlife, and plant resources and their habitats within the United States for the benefit of present and future generations of Americans."

Comment: Alternative D should be the preferred alternative. (Marine Conservation Biology Institute)

Service Response: While alternative D may be preferable from a conservation standpoint, it is not practical either logistically or financially to implement this management regime within the 15-year lifespan of this plan.

Comment: Hopefully more funds could make options 3 or 4 possible but at the very least option 2 is good. (K. Stender)

Service Response: We will use an adaptive management approach over the life of this plan. If additional funds unexpectedly become available, strategies and activities identified in alternatives C and D could be implemented.

Comment: I support Alternative B with the addition that management responsibilities should extend from the shoreline seaward to 100 fathoms to cover all coral associated with each island. These three islands should be no-take marine protected areas. (B. Carmen)

Service Response: We appreciate your support and the CCP does implement a no-take marine protected area management regime. In addition, the seaward boundary of the refuge is beyond the 100 fathom depth contour around the island. Therefore, all of the coral reefs at Howland Island are fully protected in accordance with the provisions of the National Wildlife Refuge System Administration Act of 1966, as amended.

Comment: The Final CCPs should include a more specific provision for reevaluation. (Marine Conservation Biology Institute)

Service Response: The Department of the Interior and the Service support the use of adaptive management to address uncertainty associated with implementing conservation activities. The "learning by doing" inherent in implementing activities in this CCP is central to re-evaluating the effectiveness of these activities and determining the need for management interventions to achieve the six goals identified in this plan.

2. Wilderness Review

Comment: We request that the Service analyze the wilderness resources in the CCP. (The Wilderness Society)

Service Response: The Service completed a Wilderness Review for Howland Island NWR and it is found in Appendix F of the CCP.

Comment: The CCP must also address management of both potential and designated wilderness lands in the CCP. (The Wilderness Society)

Service Response: The wilderness study area for Howland Island NWR identified in the CCP will be managed to ensure its wilderness character is not adversely impacted by implementing the management activities in the CCP.

Comment: The CCP should examine and outline a plan for off-road vehicle use. (The Wilderness Society)

Service Response: Off-road vehicle use has not been determined to be a compatible use on the refuge and is currently prohibited.

Comment: NMFS recommends that any wilderness-related management action requiring consideration and collaboration between our two agencies by fully described at the earliest opportunity.

Service Response: The Service will notify NMFS at such time that we decide to move forward in preparing a wilderness study report and associated Legislative Environmental Impact Statement for Howland Island NWR.

3. Climate Change

Comment: We believe that the Service should take a proactive approach and identify specific climate change concerns and formulate appropriate management strategies. (The Wilderness Society)

Service Response: We have included an objective in the CCP to increase understanding of impacts of global climate change by working with other agencies or institutions to conduct baseline global climate change investigations at this refuge.

Comment: The impacts of climate change were not adequately considered in the CCP. (Center for Biological Diversity)

Service Response: New information that has recently emerged on this issue has been added to the CCP.

Comment: Looks like the refuges would be an ideal but remote location to study climate change on reefs as a control. (K. Stender)

Service Response: We agree.

4. Commercial Fishing and Jurisdictional Issues

Comment: The treatment of commercial fishing and jurisdictional issues in these draft CCPs is incomplete. Each CCP should explain the processes and coordination necessary to achieve any management regime applicable to federal fisheries. (National Marine Fisheries Service)

Service Response: The "Refuge Establishment" section of the CCP has been revised to clearly indicate that the National Wildlife Refuge System Administration Act of 1966, as amended requires that the U.S. Fish and Wildlife Service maintain sole and exclusive management authority over all national wildlife refuge areas. At Howland Island NWR, the refuge includes the island and the surrounding waters out to the 3-nautical mile boundary depicted in Figure 1.2. The CCP clearly indicates that the refuge will remain closed to all public uses, including commercial fishing. The information in Appendix G pertaining to the Magnuson-Stevens Fisheries Management and Conservation Act has been revised to clearly identify the jurisdiction of the NMFS to regulate commercial fishing outside of the refuge boundary and the requirement that this Act must conform to other applicable laws, including the National Wildlife Refuge System Administration Act of 1966, as amended.

Comment: NMFS would like a more detailed description of FWS activities to assist the Department of State in negotiating a United States position on managing commercial fishing in the U.S. Exclusive Economic Zones adjacent to the Pacific Remote Insular Areas. (National Marine Fisheries Service)

Service Response: We have clarified language and provided more detail in the document that it was the Department of the Interior who notified the Department of State about a request from the

Republic of Kiribati to conduct commercial fishing in the U.S. Exclusive Economic Zone surrounding Baker Island, Howland Island, and Jarvis Island.

Comment: We have no record of a personal communication between Kitty Simonds and Jim Maragos regarding informal consultation that WESPAC continues to honor Service jurisdiction and authorities within the 3nmi offshore boundary of the refuge. Please provide that to us for our records. (Western Pacific Regional Fisheries Management Council)

Service Response: Dr. Maragos continues to maintain that such a discussion took place with Ms. Kitty Simonds although a "record of a personal communication" was not prepared or filed. We have removed this reference from the document and clarified the legal basis for U.S. Fish and Wildlife Service jurisdiction to mange the 3-nautical mile territorial seas surrounding Howland Island in conjunction with the National Wildlife Refuge System Administration Act of 1966, as amended.

Comment: The Council's Coral Reef Fisheries Management Plan needs to be included in your list of FMPs so as to provide complete information to readers and decision-makers. (Western Pacific Regional Fisheries Management Council)

Service Response: In Appendix G, we have included the plan for coral reef species in the list of commercial fisheries plans developed in accordance with the Magnuson-Stevens Fisheries Conservation and Management Act.

Comment: The statement that "commercial fishing under the auspices of any of the FMPs is not being pursued outside the 3 nmi boundary of the refuge" is erroneous and needs to be corrected.

Service Response: This was a typographical error. The statement has been revised to read that "Available information indicates commercial fishing under the auspices of any of the FMPS is not and cannot be pursued within the 3 nmi boundary of the refuge."

Written Comments Received on the Draft CCP/EA

Comment	Signatory	Organization
Letter	William L. Robinson	National Marine Fisheries Service
Letter	Shaye Wolf	Center for Biological Diversity
Letter	Keiko Bonk	Marine Conservation Biology Institute
Letter	Maribeth Oakes	The Wilderness Society
Email		Western Pacific Regional Fishery Management Council
Email	Brent Carmen	
Email	pandora2@earthlink.net	
Email	Keoki Stender	
Email	b.s achau	

www.ingramcontent.com/pod-product-compliance
Lightning Source LLC
Chambersburg PA
CBHW081221280526
45787CB00006B/2469